Is Korea
the Next Japan?

Is Korea the Next Japan?

Understanding the Structure, Strategy, and Tactics of America's Next Competitor

T. W. Kang

THE FREE PRESS
A Division of Macmillan, Inc.
NEW YORK

Collier Macmillan Publishers
LONDON

The Free Press
A Division of Macmillan, Inc.
866 Third Avenue, New York, N.Y. 10022

Collier Macmillan Canada, Inc.

Printed in the United States of America

printing number

1 2 3 4 5 6 7 8 9 10

Library of Congress Cataloging-in-Publication Data

Kang, T. W.
    Is Korea the next Japan? : understanding the structure, strategy, and tactics of America's next competitor/T. W. Kang.
        p.   cm.
    ISBN 0-02-916692-6
    1. Industry and state—Korea (South) 2. Industry and state—Japan. 3. Korea (South)—Industries. 4. Japan—Industries.
5. Korea (South)—Commerce—United States. 6. United States—Commerce—Korea (South) I. Title.
HD3616.K853K36   1989
338.9519'5—dc19   88–20315
                                                              CIP

To my parents, Ha Koo Kang and Sung In Kim,
who had the foresight to give me an international education.

Contents

Preface

Until recently Korea was known chiefly for the Korean War. In the view of most Westerners, Koreans could be grouped with any of half a dozen other Asian peoples. Indeed, when I first went to the United States about a decade and a half ago, people guessed that I was Chinese or Japanese, but never that I was Korean.

Today Korea is emerging both as a nation distinct from Japan and the other Asian countries and as the major new industrial force on the Pacific Rim—preempting the markets for steel and shipbuilding and making important inroads into the semiconductor and automobile industries.

This thrust combined with publicity related to the Seoul Olympics and the relative appreciation of the Japanese yen following the G5 agreement in September of 1985 are bringing much visibility to Korea. In particular, the appreciation of the Japanese yen had Americans and Japanese flocking to Korea (among other newly industrializing economies) for contract manufacturing. Various U.S. periodicals have featured Korea on their covers. Even in Japan, where as recently as 1983 it was difficult to find a single book on Korean business, entire sections of bookstores are devoted to the subject. Japanese newspapers run articles on Korea nearly every day. And recently, when I went to a party in Tokyo attended by high-level Japanese businessmen, I was asked many questions about the Korean economy, how to do business in Korea, and so forth.

Considering the amount of interest in Korea, I was surprised that I could not find a "business book" about Korea on the shelves of American bookstores. There are many academic books on the Korean economy, but none of them cater to the knowledge needs of the Western businessman or -woman.

Many Westerners have made or are considering making deals with the Koreans. Many of these people have had experience dealing with the Japanese, hence it is easy to make Japanese analogies when dealing with the Koreans. It is equally easy to think that the Koreans are totally different from the Japanese. Neither of these extremes is true, however. In terms of Korean versus Japanese business, it is crucial to understand where the similarities and the differences lie.

Specifically, this book deals with the admittedly somewhat delicate questions Western businesspeople ask about Korea—for example, "Why do Americans generally feel more comfortable in Korea than they do in Japan?" I have heard many American businesspeople remark on this. Chapter 1, therefore, compares and contrasts the cultures of Korea and Japan from a business perspective.

A major concern of Westerners is whether the Korean government and its policies help or hinder the foreign businessperson. It is no secret that many obstacles confront a newcomer to Korea. Chapter 2 compares Korea's government policies to those of Japan, which have come under

increasing criticism. Chapter 3 discusses the Korean economy, the result of the government policies described in
chapter 2. While some of this may be familiar to the reader,
the hope is that the chapter will provide a useful perspective which will form the basis for discussion later in the
book.

Knowledge of the structure, motives, strategy, and tactics of large Korean businesses is fundamental for anyone
partnering or competing with the Koreans. This is the
focus of chapter 4 (also discussed are some things that
Koreans do especially well). Chapter 5 extends this discussion into the newly controversial realm of high-tech industries.

An outgrowth of the comparison between the Koreans
and the Japanese is a discussion of the economic relationship between the two countries. Is there any merit in the
American perception that the Koreans hate the Japanese
and vice versa? Many Western enterprises have relationships with the Japanese and, in addition, have or are considering forming partnerships with the Koreans. Chapter
6 sheds light on some assumptions about the "love-hate"
relationship between Korea and Japan.

As Western enterprises gain experience dealing with
the Koreans as partners, they have become aware of some
of the unique problems in such arrangements. Chapter
7 considers Korean firms as partners to American firms.
What should foreign businesspeople be concerned about
when they deal in Korea or with the Koreans?

Last, Chapter 8 makes some projections about what is
in store for Korea. These center on the fact that Korea
will have to compete in global markets already dominated
by the major industrialized nations. Specifically, the trilateral relationship among the U.S., Japan, and Korea is
looked at in some detail. This should certainly be of concern to those who are thinking of anything more than
short-term involvement with the Koreans.

One of the side benefits of some of the comparative thinking about Korea and Japan is a new perspective on Japan. Until now Japan has been analyzed in the West as a singular Oriental nation. In fact, a strong case can be made that Japan is the maverick Asian nation rather than the norm. Through such a comparison, readers can judge for themselves what the relative perspective on Japan ought to be.

It is clear that unless major discontinuities occur, which is admittedly possible, partnerships between Western and Korean firms will increase significantly from year to year. Many of the problems American firms have with Japanese firms stem, for example, from the fact that neither side took the trouble to eradicate faulty assumptions from their perceptions of the other. Thus, as Korea gains visibility, I would be glad if this book represents a minuscule step toward intelligent and knowledgeable thinking about my country.

As with any endeavor of this sort, I received much support from various individuals. While it is impossible to thank all those who helped in subtle but significant ways, I would like to express my appreciation to Professors Robert H. Hayes and Dennis Encarnation of the Harvard Business School; Bill Davidow of Mohr-Davidow Ventures; my friends Ji Hong Kim and Mark Fuccio, who made constructive comments on the manuscript; Robert Wallace of The Free Press; Robert Markel, who offered his generous help all along the way; my friends at Intel; and finally, my parents, who showed much patience during the writing of this book.

1

Background:
Is Korea More Like Japan
or the United States?

ENVIRONMENT

Many American businesspeople who have been to both
Japan and Korea tell me that they have felt much more
comfortable dealing in the latter nation. This is quite puz-
zling, of course, as both of these nations share the same
Oriental heritage, including many long-held values. How
can two countries separated only by a narrow strait be
viewed so differently?

Fate tends to play very interesting games in the way
countries develop. The physical characteristics of Japan—
a small island with little arable, inhabitable land and few
natural resources relative to the United States—clearly
had a profound impact on the culture that reinforced
the Japanese development strategy. The ramifications of
the lingering effects of Japanese history, as contrasted
with that of the United States, also played a significant
role in determining the mind-set that country took on.

In this light, Korea's characteristics—very distinct from those of Japan and the United States—can also be argued to have been deeply influenced by environmental and historical factors.

The United States is practically a continent by itself; Japan is an island, and Korea is a peninsula situated between two neighboring countries. I never realized how physically big the United States was until I traversed all three thousand miles of it in my automobile. The major differences between the United States and the other two nations in this regard are quite clear: sheer size and the availability of natural resources—points already excessively belabored. While South Korea is smaller than Japan in landmass, when both countries are compared to the United States, they are in the same ballpark. And they share the same problem of a lack of useful land and natural resources. These are the decisive factors that made the Korean government adopt many aspects of the economic development strategies of the Japanese.

Though it may be considered a subtlety, the difference between an island and a peninsula situated between two countries is in fact not so trivial. An island is physically quite impervious to attack and, as a result, the culture of neighboring nations tends not to be forced on a country such as Japan. During the course of its history, Japan had ample occasion to examine foreign cultures (through cultural emissaries) and choose what to acquire and adapt. By the same token, infiltration is something about which an insular nation tends to become very sensitive. In the United States, it was only after a number of major industries had been deeply penetrated by the Japanese that national attention started to focus on that issue. In Japan, Korean products currently have a minuscule presence, yet red flags are going up everywhere.

This is not the case in a country like Korea. Korea had a much lower degree of freedom with respect to the cultural values that were imposed on it than did Japan. Korea is called the land of the morning calm, but this description is quite ironic for a country that has had continuous foreign invasions and internal revolutions. Relatively speaking, Korea could choose neither what cultural values to inherit nor how to inherit them. To my mind, this is where the cultural divergence between Korea and Japan begins.

Instability clearly plays a key role in this environment. Many of Japan's social practices originated far back in history; there is obviously much debate as to how far. However, what is clear is that the more than two centuries of relative stability and isolation that Japan enjoyed during the Tokugawa era (from around 1600) are unique in world history. In Japan today, Tokugawa Ieyasu is the most admired shogun from both a strategic and a managerial perspective. Indeed, he was an outstanding individual. Yet one could argue that many of the problems that Japan is experiencing in trying to internationalize have their roots in the policies that he put in place. And the Japanese have become exceedingly good at thriving in a stable environment. By the same token, an unstable environment drives the Japanese crazy. During the instability of exchange rates between the dollar and the yen that occurred between September of 1985 and the middle of 1987, Japanese companies were constantly replanning; as a result, they pleaded that stability of exchange rates is much more important than its absolute level. The Japanese are conditioned by history either not to change or to change in a slow and orderly manner, preserving the various interdependent elements of their society.

Korea was never afforded the luxury of a long period of stability, and as a result inherited a very different kind of outlook. While no one inherently likes the uncertainty associated with instability, one does get used to such an environment. One learns to accept change at the pace at which it is imposed and tries endlessly to turn it to one's advantage. And many of the historical interactions between the Koreans and their neighbors have made coexistence with foreigners an unavoidable reality. This may be one of the many reasons why American businesspeople feel more comfortable in that environment.

THE CONCEPT OF CULTURAL DISTANCE

When one looks at cross-cultural factors, perhaps what may be called cultural distance is important. For example, from the standpoint of cultural distance, Europe lies quite close to the United States. European languages are fairly closely related to English; European religions are practically the same; and, indeed, the ancestors of many Americans came to the United States from Europe. While there are many aspects of American culture that differ from its European counterparts, such as the emphasis placed on tradition, European culture is quite understandable to Americans. This is one of the reasons why American business has been relatively more successful in the European marketplace than in the Far East, which is culturally more distant from the United States than is Europe.

Two countries that are more culturally distant than Europe are English-speaking former Western colonies: Hong Kong and Singapore. Both have been or are British colonies, and they became free ports where cultural interaction could take place. It is obvious that Americans feel quite comfortable in such an environment. Singapore is a nation where different races and religions coexist in a way that is somewhat similar to that prevalent in the United States.

Korea and Taiwan are two newly industrializing economies that I would rate as being yet culturally further from the United States than Hong Kong and Singapore. Taiwan became a separate nation in 1949 and carries many of the traditions that are an integral part of Chinese culture. Korea, although sovereign for a much longer period, is a homogeneous society that, like Taiwan, believes strongly in Oriental culture. These two countries are heavily influenced by Confucianism and Buddhism—Christianity came into Korea only quite recently. However, Korea has been exposed to foreign influence on a multitude of occasions, and its effects still are visible today. For example, many Korean scholars have studied in the United States, speak English quite fluently, and even identify with some American values. While Korea is not quite as easy for the Americans to understand from a cultural standpoint as Hong Kong or Singapore, where English is a way of life, communication is easier compared with Japan, for example.

Among the economically influential countries of the Orient, Japan is probably the most culturally distant from the United States. Japan is also influenced by Confucian, Buddhist, and Shintoist values—Christianity is a minuscule minority. The Japanese, despite their efforts to learn English, are not motivated to develop their English capability for fear that they will become outcasts of their own society. In fact, today many key Japanese managers are unable to communicate in English and often have to labor through the rather imperfect process of working with an interpreter. The years of isolation and stability have solidified the bonds of community relationships to such a degree that it is much more difficult for the Japanese person naturally to accept foreign thoughts, behaviors, and values.

This is quite obviously my own view, and many will probably take issue with it. However, I will endeavor to support the view that Korea is culturally closer to the United States than Japan through more specific discussion comparing the two business cultures in detail. At the end of this process, the ultimate judgment is left to the reader.

THE BUSINESS CULTURES
OF KOREA AND JAPAN

Religious Influence on Business Values

From the standpoint of cultural distances, the largest discontinuity occurs when we cross over from the Occiden-

tal to the Oriental cultures. To set the stage, we should
first understand some of the elements of Oriental religion
as it relates to business.

At the risk of oversimplification—since there is much
that differentiates Korea from Japan—I will give only a
brief introductory description of religious influence here.
On the surface, both countries have practiced Confucianism and Buddhism. Shintoism is a uniquely Japanese religion, and needless to say, Korea has much more Christian
influence today than Japan does.

While Confucian influence is significant in both Korea
and Japan, Confucianism is not actively practiced today.
In this respect it is a bit like Latin, whose influence on
today's Western languages is large, yet no one speaks it
anymore. With this in mind, let's look at the statistics a
little. Korea's total population is around 40 million—about
11 million people (28.3 percent) are Buddhist, and about
9 million (23 percent) are Christian. Compare this to Japan,
whose total population is about 120 million—about 87
million people (73.9 percent) are Buddhist, and approximately 1.4 million (1.1 percent) are Christian. One has
to be a bit careful with these numbers as many Japanese
(more specifically, about 70 percent of the population)
would claim dual religions, namely, Buddhism and Shintoism. Nevertheless, one can see that Buddhist influence is
much stronger in Japan than it is in Korea.

In the West we talk much about the separation of religion
from the state. Of the religions mentioned above, Confucianism is perhaps the one that is most strongly related
to the state. Confucian influence came most from the
power of the state, as there were no formal places of wor-
ship such as temples or churches. Buddhism is said to
have come to Korea in about the fourth century, and to
Japan in about the sixth. While both nations adopted Confucianism, Korea suppressed Buddhism on a number of
occasions in its history. Thus, relatively speaking, it makes
sense that Japan has stronger Buddhist influence, and
Korea has stronger Confucian and Christian influence.

Confucianism flourished in conjunction with a strong centralized government. Today, when one looks at the trade situation, particularly between countries like Korea and Japan versus the United States, one finds a significant difference that arises from Korea and Japan having centralized government and businesses and the United States having relatively decentralized government and businesses. Both Korea and Japan have industrial policies; in the United States only Department of Defense–related policies come close to such a concept. And on the whole, both Korea and Japan tend to have much larger concentrations of industry than does the United States.

Given this centralized structure, the values of Confucianism operate fairly consistently. The concept of the family is relevant to the organizational philosophy of the Oriental firm and is probably the origin of the paternalistic aspects of many firms. The familial structure has a clear pecking order. The father is the head of the household, as the president of the company is to the firm. The first son is clearly next in line; the people higher on the totem pole and higher in age deserve respect. Clearly, the value placed on experience and job titles reflects this tendency.

While an exhaustive discussion of Confucianism is not possible here, I'd like to touch lightly on two aspects of this religion that may be pertinent. Scholarship is one. In Confucianism being a scholar entails a rather prestigious status. The intensity with which the Japanese study certain phenomena is mind-boggling. In my view the Koreans also share this tendency. A case could be made that the fervent importance that the Koreans place on the value of a Ph.D—relative to the Japanese, who are much less fanatical about Ph.Ds—shows a stronger Korean emphasis on scholarship compared with the Japanese emphasis on applied knowledge.

Another important aspect of Confucianism is the emphasis placed on effort. Working hard is valued immensely, meaning that the actual process of being industrious is as important as the result. Although there are many regions of the United States in which hard work is valued, my experience is that American firms tend to be much more results-oriented. In many Oriental firms, effort is a very important part of the performance-appraisal process, and poor results despite best effort draw a certain sympathy from the organization. Obviously, there is much more to Confucianism, but this gives us a base from which to begin to consider some of the more specific differences between Korean and Japanese business practices.

Let's turn a bit to Buddhism, by which Japanese society seems to be more influenced. Some values are at odds with what we are used to in the West. The first is that of continual refinement toward enlightenment, a goal that is very difficult to achieve on this earth. In this sense nothing is permanent or absolute. One is reminded of quality programs in Japanese factories, where no one is ever satisfied with the current quality levels. In a sense the goal of zero defects is as elusive as enlightenment in Buddhism. Contrast this to the United States—where motivation and satisfaction, in the form of positive feedback to keep one going, are expected. In Japan, one can start in the martial arts and never get positive feedback for ten years. Likewise, in the corporate context, developing a new customer in Japan usually requires a long period of endurance without positive feedback in the form of profitable orders.

Greed and ego are vices in the Buddhist religion. One could facetiously say that these aspects are the very factors that drive entrepreneurs in Silicon Valley. Harmony is virtuous in Buddhism. American society operates on healthy confrontation between different and heterogeneous interest groups. The middle path, which Buddhism encourages as an alternative to extremes, is at times at odds with American corporate policy. I have seen many examples in corporate America of policy shifting like a pendulum—which in the positive sense means adaptability. According to Buddhism, emotion and passion are things that get in the way of the purity of the mind. These are the very aspects that Westerners complain about when discussing or negotiating with the Japanese—they cannot read the Japanese mind. And while we are on the subject of the mind, the Buddhist religion clearly states that wisdom comes as a result of mind control rather than analysis, which is supposed to be more confusing than it is guiding. The relatively intuitive nature of the Japanese managers' decision-making process perhaps has something to do with this.

It's clear that this sketchy characterization of some of the Buddhist values seems much more aligned with the image of the Japanese culture today than with the Korean. Again, if the assumption is correct that Buddhist influence is much stronger in Japan than in Korea, and that Christian influence is much stronger in Korea than in Japan, it seems logical that the Japanese value system would be more distant from that of the United States than the Korean value system.

Individualism versus Team Orientation

To anyone who has worked with both Korean and Japanese businessmen, it is quite natural to believe that the Koreans tend to be more individualistic than the Japanese. Despite this appearance, one cannot honestly fault the Koreans for poor teamwork. Many Korean companies have taken on projects that require coordination between various groups of people and executed them fairly well. In order to really understand this phenomenon, one must look at the two issues somewhat separately.

I once heard a Japanese academic remark: "I would grudgingly admit that if you pit an excellent Korean against an excellent Japanese, the Korean would probably win. However, once you put a team of five together on both sides, I can guarantee you that the Japanese would win hands down." Interestingly, this is a comment that has also been made about the Americans vis-à-vis the Japanese.

Let's try to put two previously mentioned factors together. In Confucianism, the family-community occupies a very important place in society. Both the Koreans and the Japanese are family-community oriented. But instability drives the Koreans to behave very differently in this regard. Imagine that just as one starts to make friends with people in one's community, instability disorients the community. It isn't surprising that in this type of climate one looks out for number one and the family. In addition, in the quest for a sense of belonging, Koreans tend to associate themselves with those who come from their home province, and those with whom they went to school. Thus a Korean organization is made up of a heterogeneous network of family, school, and home-province ties. Contrast this to Japan, where in agricultural communities, a long period of stability fostered a kind of interdependence between different families that led to quite an efficient division of labor. This is the approximate origin of the Japanese concept of *mura* ("village"), and the village is sometimes more important than the family from the viewpoint that deviance cuts one off from an important network of dependencies. This partially explains why employee turnover rates are significantly higher in Korean enterprises compared to its Japanese counterparts.

In Japan, where a community tends to remain stable for a long period of time, people tend to understand the value, strengths, and weaknesses of others in the community. In Korea, where this stability is somewhat of a luxury, few people would probably understand or accept a person's potential, and as a result, the only way to get ahead and prosper is to oversell oneself. Thus, the ego and pride that the Koreans seem to have are used constantly to remind others of one's accomplishments. Clearly, here the individual stands high on the list of priorities.

One of the competing forces within many Korean organizations is the trade-off between this individualism and what might be called a top-down management style. In many Korean firms, the Confucian value of the family hierarchy—that is, higher position and experience command respect—and the militaristic aspect of Korean society, which will be discussed in more detail later, contribute to a top-down mode of operation. One reason why the Korean organization holds together despite such opposing forces is the employer-employee power balance. While the Japanese are often said to be loyal to their employers, my long experience in Japan suggests that Japanese employees conform to their employers' policies because the costs of deviance and switching to another employer are very high. In the United States, unless one is an excessive job-hopper, switching employers is considered reasonable. In Japan, combine the negative stigma attached to a person who leaves a large Japanese company with the fact that most large firms don't practice lateral hiring, and the result is that job-switching is prohibitively expensive.

In Korea, job-hopping is more acceptable, but it can be afforded only by those who are skilled. For those who aren't, the cost is even higher than in Japan. While different countries have different conventions for counting unemployment, the Japanese have been screaming that their unemployment rate has passed 3 percent. The official Korean unemployment rate is said to be around 4 percent, but in reality it is common knowledge that this number is too conservative. In Korea there are still some people who go to work in a company without pay because they need somewhere to go to save face socially and with their families. One is very fortunate to have a paying job. In this sense the Koreans are hungrier than the Japanese. They are grateful for the job they've got and will suppress their personal inclinations to keep it. This is the glue that holds the top-down-driven firms together despite the individuality of the people.

The Koenchanayo *Spirit versus Detail Orientation, Planning, and Long-Term Thinking*

Japanese people who have done business in Korea are often intrigued by the Korean expression *koenchanayo*. Quite complex to translate, it literally means "that's all right," "that's good enough," or "that's about right." Like many Oriental expressions, it means different things in different contexts.

In the positive sense, *koenchanayo* expresses a willingness to tolerate and appreciate other people's efforts. For example, if a person is requested to perform a favor, and that person says he or she isn't sure if the response to the request is satisfactory to the requester, then the requester allays such insecurity by saying *koenchanayo*, or "that's good enough." In the business context, if, for example, someone is requested to get a certain set of data but can only come close, the requester shows tolerance and appreciation through the use of this expression. Being big-hearted and not excessively picky is a key part of *koenchanayo*.

It is clear why the Japanese noticed this concept so quickly: This mode of thinking is awkward in Japanese industry. In Japan, where continuous progress is a way of life, things are never good enough—quality can get better, cost can be reduced further, product dimensions can be miniaturized more, and customer service can be improved upon.

One characteristic of the Japanese businessman is that he is uncompromisingly thorough. And part of the reason the Japanese have been able to be so thorough is again related to the relative stability of their society. In fact, when an oil crisis or the fluctuating dollar exchange rates require of Japanese firms repeated revision of their plans, they grumble, not realizing that the option to plan is a privilege. Korean firms have never been afforded such a luxury. In a society where changes in political power bring about chaotic upheavals in policy, in contrast to the continuity of vision that Japan's Liberal Democratic Party has maintained, one must take a very different attitude toward planning. In Korea the prevalent attitude is that there are so many unknown variables in the course of business that no amount of thorough planning can anticipate all the unforeseen circumstances. As a result, a typical Korean business venture tends to combine willpower with fatalistic optimism. The latter is described well by the expression *chumoktajim*, the Korean equivalent of "go for it." Of course, the implication here is that things will work out in the end. This is the thought process that underlies the expression *koenchanayo*. Whatever the adversity, it will have to be overcome by stepped-up effort and raw willpower. A specific manifestation of this attitude is the lack of attention paid to detail in planning. From this standpoint, to the average Japanese, the Koreans probably look somewhat absent-minded.

While it may seem excessive to harp on the theme of stability, its effect on the Korean manager's time-horizon is pronounced. The Japanese think very long-term. Their long-term strategy is ten years out—most U.S. long-range plans are five years out. The Koreans plan five years or more, but they start executing before most of the questions are answered. This is partly due to the fact that they often follow plans that have already worked in Japan or in the West. But it also has something to do with the attitude that says, "Let's get our act together and get this thing kicked off. As to what happens later, we'll cross that bridge when we get to it." For example, in the factory, the Koreans depart radically from the Japanese "do it right the first time" philosophy.

We all know that the best Japanese factories trace their faults back to the design phase and fix the origin of the problem. In my many visits to Japanese factories, I noticed that rework areas were quite small. In contrast, in many

Korean factories the "get started, see how it goes, and fix it later" type of thinking prevails. In their book *In Search of Excellence,* Peters and Waterman have called this "a bias for action," which they show is characteristic of successful firms. This also explains why the Koreans can get something done so quickly. The downside of this philosophy is that, in a number of factories I saw in the large Korean firms, there were rather substantial rework areas. In fact, one of the plants even had a rework line for rejects. What is fascinating is that despite this method of operation, these firms have been producing competitive products for a number of years. At least for now, labor costs are so low that even with these added steps, they can be rather effective. Korean televisions and other consumer appliances have been selling in the U.S. market for a good number of years under their own and private labels—there hasn't been much reporting of excessive quality problems.

Maturity of Commerce

It is interesting that the same Confucian value system held by the Japanese and the Koreans has produced two fundamentally different outlooks. Japan has for centuries placed great value on commerce. The Japanese ability to transact business in a professional manner is the result of centuries of experience, not a talent that the Japanese developed in the last forty years. Despite the fact that merchants were the lowest-ranked social class, some of the oldest firms in Japan date back to the 1600s, during the Tokugawa shogunate, when much domestic commerce was practiced by family enterprises. This family enterprise system owes much to the Confucian belief in family unity.

Korea, on the other hand, has stressed the importance of the Confucian belief in scholarship over commerce.

The Korean *yangban,* the elite and cultured top echelons of society, were clearly not commercially minded. There are no Korean firms that can trace their beginnings back to the seventeenth century as can some in Japan. So, in a sense, the Korean position in world industry today is the most remarkable example of catch-up—it has taken the Koreans such a short time to accomplish so much.

This difference is apparent in the business practices of the two countries even today. For example, the Koreans and Japanese treat customers in fundamentally different ways. The Japanese believe in a concept called *giri,* which implies that the customer will be taken care of. So, in Japan, even after money has changed hands, a lot of firms and establishments continue to give the customer his or her money's worth, thus fulfilling their *giri.* And if he or she seems dissatisfied, most trustworthy Japanese firms will try—within the boundaries of economic reasonability—to fulfill the customer's desire. So, Japanese customer treatment is largely relationship-based.

In contrast, the Korean perception of and attitude toward customers is much more transaction-based. First, the discussion centers around price—the customers know to negotiate. But, second, if one considers how much inconvenience and confusion there were during the Korean War, and how much postwar poverty, it is easy to feel that since the customer paid so little for the product or service, he or she can put up with a little inconvenience as well. In this context it is easy for the Korean firm to say that they provided approximately what they promised—another instance of *koenchanayo.* (The Japanese would say, "Close, but no cigar.") However, even with this type of philosophy, it seems that there is a rather sizable market for inexpensive products and services, not only in Korea but in the West.

Many Korean firms have recognized this and are trying very hard to catch up in the arena of customer service.

This is particularly important as, eventually, when cost differentials diminish, service levels will become an important competitive parameter.

THE EMOTIONAL FACTOR

The Koreans like Verdi; the Japanese like German lieder. I could not think of a more appropriate way to express the different attitudes that these two countries take toward emotion. A Verdi opera brings to mind a pouring-out of emotion, fancy dress, and a visually striking stage set. A Schubert song cycle such as *Die Winterreise,* on the other hand, is the epitome of poetry, subtle expression, and permits varying depths of interpretation.

When looking at Korean clothes or temples, one notices vibrant colors and outward beauty. In Japan the most valued form of beauty lies in subtlety that usually exists below the surface.

It is not generally considered correct for the Japanese to show emotion. I find it interesting, for example, that society considers it poor form for a Japanese widow to cry during her husband's funeral. On the other hand, in Korea, even when a distant relative dies, it is poor form *not* to display emotion.

This issue of whether or not to be overtly emotional has become a significant one in international relations. I hear countless times from American businesspeople that they feel uncomfortable because the Japanese often have little emotional reaction to proposals made to them. A Japanese businessperson who doesn't display emotion is considered to be shrewd in the sense that he or she is hard to read, and composed in the sense that he or she is not biased and avoids coming to a premature conclusion. Foreigners, on the other hand, tend to interpret this as clever game playing—a strategic use of the poker face.

In an outward manner, the Koreans in general tend to be fairly true to their emotions. While they tend to value composure and maturity as well, they seem to be more open to expressing reactions. This is probably one of the more important reasons why Western businesspeople are more comfortable dealing with the Koreans than the Japanese.

The word *jyo* in Japanese and the word *jung* in Korean are represented by the same Chinese character, which expresses a feeling of warmth that transfers from one person to another in a way that makes two people feel closer to one another. The concept is also related to sympathy. Even in English, the expression "I think I know how you feel" is perhaps an expression of *jyo* or *jung*. This is an Oriental concept that is rather hard to convey precisely in the English language. Yet, when someone in Korea apologizes to another person for not being able to treat that person in the proper manner, the recipient of that apology usually says *koenchanayo,* which in this context means "that's quite all right"—a beautiful use of this expression and a verbal portrayal of *jung.*

Both countries clearly share this concept, but they identify with it in very different ways. The Koreans feel that the Japanese are cold, and their politeness is only superficial. "How could one not shed tears during the funeral of one's spouse?" Yet the Japanese feel quite differently. If two people are really close, one should not have to display emotion for the other to understand the intended consideration. In fact, a display of emotion in Japan is a sign that the relationship is not really intimate.

This is quite relevant to the cultural distance idea in the following way. American society is so heterogeneous that if one could not communicate the most basic form of a logical statement—yes or no—much confusion would arise from the inability to resolve widely differing positions. Among the countries mentioned in the section on cultural distance, in this regard Japan is probably the most distant from the United States. In Japan, detecting a no answer to a Western proposal is at best a very imprecise art that becomes close to impossible when one is operating in the Nagoya or Osaka area. The Koreans are perhaps not as explicit as the Americans in asserting the negative. However, in their polite way, the signal is there. When one pays careful attention to facial expression, body language, and the words, one can usually detect a no. The main difference is that in a Korean meeting, there is usually at least one individual who either is the decision maker or feels compelled to express himself. The Japanese act in groups, and usually anyone who is inclined to be overt is motivated to stay in line.

JAPANESE *ANSHIN* VERSUS KOREAN *ANSHIM*

Both of the above words basically mean "peace of mind." They are different pronunciations of the same two Chinese characters. While it is generally true that everyone in the world desires peace of mind, there seem to be differing degrees of this need.

From my perspective, this difference in degree between the Japanese and the Koreans is borne out very clearly by looking at the frequency with which this expression is used in both countries. To anyone who has done business in Japan or Korea, it is obvious that the Japanese use this expression perhaps ten times as often as the Koreans do. They want to purchase a product or service that gives them *anshinkan*. They want to engage in relationships that foster *anshinkan*. They want business plans that ensure *anshinkan*. And they want little surprise.

The Americans, of course, opt for peace of mind, but it seems that they trade it off with a little adventurousness. American customers are willing to take a risk on a new product or concept even if it comes from a firm with little reputation or track record. American distributors are willing to try new suppliers that offer good products or services. Judging from the few times Korean businessmen seem to use this expression, they certainly take a very different outlook as compared to the Japanese. As mentioned before, their history has forced so many things on them that they don't have peace of mind, or *anshim*, to start with. Thus, they are also more apt to go for the value even if there is some risk that their sense of *anshim* may be broken. Koreans can live with surprises; they'll find a way to adjust to them when they happen.

POLITICAL FACTORS

Commenting on political affairs is very difficult, and even if it weren't, I would be the wrong person to do it. However, certain fundamental political factors have influenced the nature of the Korean people and industry.

The first of these is clearly controversial: the trade-off between authoritarianism and democracy. There is no doubt in anyone's mind that freedom is desirable. However, in a country such as the United States, where freedom is an essential part of the value system, it is difficult if not taboo even to broach the subject of the costs of unlimited freedom in the industrial arena.

First and foremost, in order for a democratic nation to be effective, the populace must be well educated. When the Koreans were recovering from the Korean War, they simply were not in a situation in which the people could optimally decide what industrial trade-offs were appropriate for the nation. And even if there had been representation at that time, it wouldn't have been very competent.

Second, as is the case with Japan, a resource-poor country must navigate through very narrow straits of tolerance in order even to have a chance to develop economically. This would mean precise and coordinated execution of a government policy at a given point in time and consistency in the implementation of that policy over a certain period of time. This is particularly important for a country like Korea, where the historical context has tended to be quite turbulent and uncoordinated endeavors would end in chaos.

In many ways Korea has chosen Japan as its role model for economic development. Obviously this approach has many advantages and disadvantages. Yet, once this determination is clear, all that is left is precise execution of an industrial policy carefully modified to fit the Korean environment. While the individual may perhaps have been sacrificed for the benefit of the country, one still wonders whether one would have chosen total freedom and poverty or limited freedom and a very visible increase in the standard of living. As will become clear in the next chapter, the key success factors in the Korean development strategy will be the timing and rate of liberation of various industrial elements and rights. Too early would mean a loss of focus and control over the steady progress that has been made. Too late could provoke retaliatory reaction from the people and trading partners.

Part of the reason why a relatively authoritarian system prevailed in Korea has to do with a second factor that needs to be mentioned: the threat from the North and military influence. The last of the many upheavals that have plagued Korea, the Korean War, left countless numbers of divided families—that is, families in which some members live in North Korea and the rest in the South. While more will be mentioned later, North Korea happens to be a country with an extreme ideology and unfortunately a significant military force to back it up.

It is often said that one of the pillars supporting the Japanese zeal in the quest for economic development was the need to survive. Japan wanted to survive industrially because it lacked natural resources and, at the time, the perception was that this was a great disadvantage for industrialization. The Korean version of this takes on a slightly different form. Korea not only has this disadvantage but shoulders the burden of having an enemy across the border only twenty-five miles from Seoul. This enemy, which encompasses relatives of some South Korean families, is one of the closest societies on earth to the Orwellian state. Putting it as objectively as possible, North Korea has clearly traded off political ideology against economic reality in quite an extreme fashion. While South Korea is economically not yet in the same ballpark as Japan, on an economic scale it dwarfs North Korea. In fact, it was reported recently that the North Koreans were in danger of defaulting on $750 million of external debt. South Korea currently has in excess of $30 billion in external debt, and recently its modest trade surplus has boosted confidence that the country would be able to service this significant debt. We shall come back to this in more detail later.

Here is an example of what is meant by navigating through narrow tolerances. Japan is called an economic miracle for being able to execute a brilliant development strategy despite resource poverty. But Japan has never spent much more than 1 percent of its GNP on defense, which goes toward the maintenance of a self-defense force. The Japanese save much more than the Korean people do, and as a result capital formation is much higher. Korea, on the other hand, maintains a full-fledged army that consumes about 5 percent of the Korean GNP. Korea had no choice but to take the risk of overextending itself on external debt, and the country seems to be able to service it. It could be argued that the Korean economic achievement is even more miraculous than Japan's from this perspective.

In South Korea, every male must by law serve approximately three years in the military—no easy task. During this duty some experience the tension of the demilitarized zone, where even today rounds of fire are exchanged. After their mandatory military duty, South Koreans are sent to *Yoebigun,* a civilian backup force that meets regularly for short but intensive training. This is probably about the best reminder there is of the need to survive. Indeed, defending the country against its northerly neighbor has resulted in some key governmental posts being filled by former high-ranking military officials. This, combined with the all-encompassing military requirement, makes for a society that operates well with top-down leadership.

This type of behavior often manifests itself in the industrial arena. The Kyeong-Bu Expressway, joining the two largest cities in South Korea, Seoul and Pusan, was built in record time—time that many non-Korean firms asserted was impossible. Seoul's underground transit system was nonexistent until the decision was made to put one in—then four lines were put in at the same time. During the construction period this created a tremendous congestion problem, since they dug up all the already-crowded streets. But in a matter of a few years, all the lines were in place, and Seoul now boasts the world's most modern subway system. Compare this to the way the Japanese put in their subway system—incrementally, one line at a time, but with attention to every detail in the construction process. The Koreans say that, coming from behind, if they had taken the same amount of time the Japanese did, they'd never have caught up. Some of the Korean firms assert that they can construct a factory in half the time it takes a Japanese company. Human endurance, speed, efficiency, and labor cost, at least for now, are important competitive advantages that they stress relative to the Japanese.

As pointed out earlier, this aggressiveness is fueled by the fact that there is no other way—that is, if they don't do it better they just won't survive. Clearly, however, as the knowledge and intelligence of the average Korean citizen improve, this fairly straightforward focus will start to wane and the country will be forced to consider trade-offs that are inherent to the overhead necessary for democratization.

What is fascinating is that with such a different culture and different heritage, the Koreans apparently realize that there are enough similarities between Japan and Korea in terms of the lack of natural resources, small area, literate population, and so on to make the Japanese model worth following as long as it works. The structure of the various government ministries, the economic-planning process, export orientation, and the focus toward large-scale industries (as opposed to Taiwan) are all examples of this. To use an analogy from the world of computers, the people are the hardware foundation on which various software is built. The Koreans are trying to make some Japanese strategies (software) run on Korean hardware (the people and culture). This is analogous to the same personal computer software (such as Lotus 1–2–3) running on both an IBM-PC and an Apple personal computer. Although execution on different hardware requires modification of the software, the end result which the user sees is the same.

So the goal for Korea is, "Do what the Japanese have done, but do it cheaper and faster."

2

Government Policies Related to International Trade

As the world becomes more and more internationally interdependent, businesspeople have no choice but to deal with governments around the world. Needless to say, government policies can promote or hinder international trade in either direction, set the parameters of domestic competition, influence financial matters, and so on. Thus it is important to understand in a certain amount of depth the effects Korea's government policies have had and what is in store for the future.

Korean government policies, particularly those that relate to trade, closely resemble those of Japan. Critics of Japan tend to look at aspects of Japanese industrial policy as hindrances to harmonious coexistence with foreign business. Extremists—some of whom are Japanese—even say that so-called Japan bashing has its roots in the "selfish" industrial policy that Japan clung to for so long. If Korea resembles Japan in this regard, will the effects be similar?

Proposing an answer requires an understanding of the similarities and differences between the two nations' policies.

THE ENVIRONMENT

Given ordinary circumstances, both Japan and Korea should have remained in absolute poverty. After all, the only resource these two nations had was an abundance of people. Though Americans can extrapolate intellectually what this means, they can scarcely understand what it feels like in reality. I know, because I almost forgot the feeling after being in the United States for almost fifteen years. I still remember the first time I encountered the word *claustrophobic* in the English language. Suffice it to say that such a phobia simply does not exist in a place like Japan or Korea, and one has no other choice but to adjust to an extremely crowded environment.

The obvious reason why Japan's development is considered to be an economic miracle is that the country was never endowed with the physical environment in which such an accomplishment would come about naturally. People had to work practically inhumane hours, the distribution system had to become complex to average out profits and keep unemployment low, and society had to tolerate such restrictions on the availability of land that the universal dream of securing a house has just about disappeared for most of the population. There is an expression that goes, "There are many ways to climb a mountain"; however, the perception has been that there were very few degrees of freedom in order to "make it." It is probably this very perception that is one of the drivers of the economic friction that exists today.

As mentioned previously, the physical characteristics that Korea has to work with are very similar to those of Japan. In addition, during the Japanese occupation of

Korea (1910–45), rightly or wrongly, the generation of Koreans that constitute top management in large Korean firms were conditioned to operate in the Japanese manner. The Koreans, of course, are still emotionally provoked when thinking about this era. Yet sometimes the psychology of oppression works in interesting ways. Much like the drill camps for the U.S. marines at Parris Island, while individuals start out hating the system, when they understand that the only way to survive is to conform, they tend subliminally to identify with the prevailing values. The simple fact that the Korean educational system is modeled on the Japanese, practically down to the textbook level, is ample evidence of this.

So, given the physical similarities and the infrastructure of values that was put into place during the occupation, the Japanese system became the model to emulate.

Similarities in the Governmental Organization of the Two Countries

While the Korean government is a presidential system and the Japanese government a prime ministerial one, the various ministries that formulate policies and regulations are practically mirror images of each other. For example, the Korean counterpart of Japan's MITI (Ministry of International Trade and Industry) is MTI, the Ministry of Trade and Industry. Korea, like Japan, also has ministries of finance, education, defense, science, technology, and so on. The Economic Planning Board (EPB) in Korea is practically the same as the Economic Planning Agency in Japan. There are also similarities in the organizational structure within the various ministries. While it is important to note that there are some differences between the two systems, such as the minister of EPB being a deputy prime minister, let us first discuss the similarities and then understand the differences later.

Similarities in Policies Used to Bootstrap the Economy into Rapid Growth

The similarity does not stop with the structure of the ministries. The policies embarked on are also analogous to their Japanese counterparts.

Export orientation: Outward-looking export emphasis became the primary engine of economic growth. The alternative is, of course, to concentrate on the domestic marketplace; however, the choice was based largely on the previously mentioned lack of natural resources, low capital accumulation, and a relatively small domestic market due to poverty.

In order to bring such a policy to fruition, various incentives were put in place to encourage the private sector to behave in a consistent manner. The basic structure of the system was such that firms that had important export volume benefited significantly over firms whose exports were lower. The number of such incentives demonstrates the zeal with which this "export or die" policy was pursued.

Firstly, there were financial subsidies. These spanned the many activities exporters must deal in: offshore procurement and import of raw materials, production, overseas marketing activities, and so on. The Export-Import Bank provided low-cost funds for export activities that required long working-capital cycles. Foreign exchange was made available at attractive terms to firms that needed to purchase foreign plant and equipment for the manufacture of export products.

Tax exemptions were also aggressively employed. Until 1973 there was direct exemption on corporate taxes. From then on indirect tax incentives included accelerated depreciation, exemption from value added tax, and exemptions on import tariffs for raw materials and spare parts. These incentives also helped domestic subcontractors and suppliers of the export firms.

Other incentives helped the actual operation of businesses. A direct example would be reduced rates on public utilities and wastage allowance subsidies. Ability to import certain goods and various monopolistic rights were tied to export performance. The president of Korea himself provided significant personal emphasis by attending Export Day, an annual event, and recognizing excellent export performance.

In retrospect, these incentives were quite effective in view of the actual growth in exports. Also, trade patterns have been changed from several points of view. The product content of export items became increasingly sophisticated, migrating originally from primary products to manufactured products. The trend followed here is also similar to that in Japan, where in the beginning labor-intensive, light-industrial goods constituted a significant part of the export volume. As time passed, this switched to heavy and chemical goods such as steel, shipbuilding, and so on, and finally Korea is moving toward the knowledge-intensive or high-technology industries. This shift in product content came mainly from economic and industrial planning. Also, until 1965, Japan was Korea's largest export market; since then the United States has had that "distinction."

Economic planning: Korea is now in the midst of its sixth five-year economic plan. These plans are formulated largely by the Economic Planning Board. The organization spans a broad range of activities: overall planning, infrastructure development, social development, current economic research, external relations planning, and financial planning. The formulation of each five-year plan takes around two years, and environmental changes are taken into account through updates in the plans. This economic orchestration is then forwarded to the various ministries for implementation planning. The Ministry of Trade and Industry, for example, is responsible for trade-sector planning. Specific industry plans are formulated by industry associations whose private-sector membership works in close cooperation with the ministries.

There is some disagreement over whether these plans

anticipate or react to the economic environment. Government officials claim that the long-term nature of such activities as the development of industrial infrastructure and scientific knowledge require foresight, and that the Japanese development experience helped Korea to anticipate these needs. However, the corporate-planning director of a major conglomate said, "The EPB people are nothing more than sophisticated extrapolators. When a private sector company finds success in a particular industry or product area, the planners just write up the success formula and call that a plan. Also, most of the environmental inputs to their plans come from us after the fact."

As is the case with Japan, the earlier Korean five-year plans tended to be much more successful than the later ones. The usual explanation one gets for this is that the earlier plans were "control" plans that were legally enforced, whereas the later ones were "indicative" ones that were enforced more by bureaucratic than by legal influence. Of course, the role of government and the relationship between the public and private sectors are closely related to this.

Big business and government support: Relative to other newly industrializing economies, Korea has chosen the path of maximizing capital concentration. Big business dominates the Korean economy—the top five conglomerates account for approximately half of the national output. The reason for this inclination is obviously scale-related—that capital-intensive industries will benefit from the efficiency caused by large production volumes and a concentration of capital. And, in order to achieve peak efficiency, it was important to gain scale in a short period of time, meaning emphasis on growth over profits.

While we shall cover this topic in more detail later, Korean conglomerates called *chaebol*—whose Chinese characters in Japanese are read *zaibatsu*—are somewhat similar to the Japanese groups. They cover a broad range of products and services, they aggressively perform hybrid pricing, and they establish both financial and trade relationships between various firms within the group so that synergy is maximized. There are nonetheless some subtle differences, which we shall discuss in more detail in the next chapter.

This rate of capital concentration would not have taken place had there not been support from the government. The predominant view in government was that big business was going to have the highest probability of success abroad, and as a result many of the export incentives were primarily available for big business. When adding up such financial incentives, much credit had selectively become available at incredibly low costs of capital. As a result, a growth-oriented policy naturally resulted in quite aggressive leverage ratios, even in comparison with some of the debt-aggressive Japanese firms. For example, some Korean firms carry a debt-equity ratio in excess of 6:1.

One critical difference in the execution of this development strategy is that financing growth has been even more difficult for Korea than for Japan, even with very dramatic growth in the money supply. This resulted in general interest rates that are exceedingly high, and in certain nonpreferential industry sectors becoming starved for capital. It is important to note also that capital formation in Korea is not as powerful as in Japan, where the savings rate is much higher. The short-term attitudes of the Korean people, mentioned in the previous chapter, led them to consume more relative to the Japanese. And, as mentioned earlier, defense expenditures—which constitute nearly 40 percent of the government budget, or 5 percent of GNP—produced an explosive need for funds. It is well known that Japan has consistently spent less than 1 percent of its GNP on defense. Hence the shortfall in capital needs had to come from foreign sources, which led to a cumulative foreign debt in excess of $30 billion. Korea has just recently got to the point where the interest on this debt can be serviced and its debt somewhat reduced through trade-balance surpluses, which some Western economists argue is why Korea should be allowed to earn foreign exchange through export. As recently as the early 1980s, foreign creditors were nervous about Korean liquidity. So, it is clear that Korea had to take a much higher financial risk than did Japan to pursue a similar strategy.

The general thrust of the Japanese development strategy—export orientation, focus on big business, and economic planning—is carried through in the Korean case as well. In addition, the aspects of Japanese policy that are controversial to its trading partners, namely import restrictions, capital controls, and controls on foreign exchange, are also emulated in the Korean policies.

*Similarities in Policies That Endeavor to Establish
International Harmony*

When one looks at the Korean and Japanese experiences, some elements of their strategies have caused considerable grief to foreign businesspeople. The Japanese and Korean domestic markets have been perceived to be closed to foreign suppliers through a combination of tariff and nontariff barriers. Foreign exchange controls prohibited repatriation of funds even if one was successful abroad. There is also tough competition in their own backyards, due perhaps to the export drive that has gone on. These are the obvious problems among many that demonstrate the structural differences between countries. These problems have recently caused the Japanese a lot of pain, and as a result, considerable thought must be given to whether a straightforward following of the Japanese model is going to continue to work.

Starting in the seventies, the Japanese embarked on a direction that would endeavor to pacify some of these foreign frustrations. The Koreans are also following in these footsteps. They include:

Import liberalization: Every year the number of items subject to import tariffs has gone down. But clearly the rate of liberalization has been quite slow, as any visitor who had the misfortune of carrying a foreign consumer appliance into Kimpo Airport customs is painfully aware. While this is obviously a first step, as is the case in Japan, the debate still remains even after the products make it into Korea tax-free. The issue is nontariff barriers, and it is sure to be the topic of a great deal of discussion in the future.

Foreign capital–technology inducement and limited relaxation of foreign exchange limitations: As mentioned earlier, given Korea's enormous need for funds, the formula had to be to earn as much foreign exchange as possible through exports, to minimize foreign exchange outflow through capping availability of foreign goods in the local marketplace, and also to halt outflow of foreign exchange from the country in general. For example, until 1987, if a Korean family sent a child abroad, there was a very modest cap on how much money in foreign exchange could be sent to the child on a monthly basis. Needless to say, repatriation of funds by a Korean subsidiary of a foreign firm to the parent company in the form of dividends was very restricted. As described before, even with these severe limitations, Korean external debt had ballooned to nearly $40 billion by the mid-eighties and the serviceability of this debt is not a certainty yet.

Recently, however, the government is allowing some relaxation of these controls in order to attract foreign capital and technology. A limited allowance of dividend repatriation abroad is an example. Another financial incentive is that corporate taxes are exempted for a foreign subsidiary if that subsidiary meets certain criteria—that is, for example, the foreign firm brings "unique" technology into

Korea, or the foreign firm builds a plant in Korea that exports more than half of its output. There are numerous other relaxations that relate to ownership structure of foreign investment in Korea. Depending on the industry, a foreign firm could not own a majority interest in a Korean operation; this is changing quickly, however, and according to industry priority. Also, partnerships between Korean and foreign firms formerly had to be approved by the Ministry of Finance and the Ministry of Commerce and Industry (the forerunner of MTI), which in itself proved to be a rather lengthy process. And even if negotiations with a Korean firm were near closure, there remained the possibility that the government would create different expectations on the terms and conditions of the cooperative. In recent years, however, the approval methodology has changed to a negative list system; that is, unless a potential partnership fits a specific set of criteria that the government wants to pay attention to, the approval cycle is quasi-automatic, although it is still clear that the government is involved in some fashion.

Stronger enforcement of intellectual property: Anyone who has been to Itaewon, the Seoul shopping district most popular with foreigners, knows how much selling of knock-off merchandise goes on. Foreign firms that have large intellectual property content, in the form of either brands, trademarks, patents, or copyrights, would rightfully feel uncomfortable investing in Korea. As a result the Korean government has enacted several regulations that provide stricter protection of intellectual property and fewer restrictions on the terms under which one can license such property. In the past the Korean government required a know-how transfer from the foreign firm to the Korean firm as a condition for the ability to license that know-how to the Korean firm. Now, straight licensing is possible.

Export restraints: Japan's overaggressive export policies have come under strong criticism, and it is becoming more and more clear that export markets will not tolerate massive trade deficits against Japan on a continuing basis. Korea has certainly been at least partially subject to these same pressures. There has been talk and action recently about setting voluntary restraints on exports to the United States in the form of either restricting the volume of export or establishing a price floor for exported goods in a certain product category. Korea is also trying to balance and diversify its trading partners—whether by diversification away from Japan in imports or diversification away from the United States in exports.

Upgrading the industrial base: While Korea has had a labor-cost advantage for a number of years, it is becoming increasingly apparent that other countries with even lower labor costs are becoming competitive and attractive to foreign firms. As a result Korean government and industry are trying aggressively to shift their product base to higher-value-added products. These are high-tech or knowledge-intensive products. It took the Japanese a long time to set up the infrastructure to establish the foundation for such an orientation. The reason for this is that these higher-value-added activities require mature and experienced human resources that—unlike sheer labor, capital, or even technology—cannot be acquired instantaneously. This will be covered later in some more detail.

Support of small- and medium-size businesses: Mention was made of the high concentration of capital in Korea. This policy is quite effective when one considers scale; however, from an employment standpoint, there is a limit to this approach. For example, in Korea the top thirty conglomerates employ on the order of a quarter of the employable labor pool. Japan has been able to control its unemployment rate through the existence of small-to-medium-size firms that serve as suppliers and sales channels for big business. And, based on the U.S. experience, much innovation has come from entrepreneurial endeavors that are only possible in the absence of excessive red tape, and that type of strength must be harbored in order for Korea to join the ranks of the advanced nations. Some of the assistance provided to smaller-scale businesses includes funding, technical assistance, assistance in formation of partnerships with foreign firms, reserving business segments for small businesses, and interlocking small and medium-size businesses with big business as has been done in Japan.

Some Differences Between the Korean and Japanese Systems

Despite the similarities, both countries like to feel that their systems are quite distinct and, in fact, they are in certain ways.

Degrees of freedom given to bureaucrats and their capabilities: I mentioned that the structure within the ministries was similar in both countries. The line of command runs from the minister to vice minister to bureau chiefs to section managers. However, structure is only one aspect of how organizations run. One manifestation of this is that in Japanese ministries, the only politically appointed persons are indeed the top man—the minister himself—and perhaps one other person who serves as a liaison to the political world. The rest of the bureaucrats are career officials, many of them veterans in industrial issues. Promotions within the management hierarchy are quite competitive and are generally on the basis of "up or out." Therefore, while the minister has political power, all the knowledge power that is crucial to the implementation of a given policy is in the hands of the bureaucrats.

In Korea, on the other hand, a somewhat different system is in place. In Korean ministries, not only is the minister appointed politically, but sometimes such appointments run down to the bureau-chief level. As a result bureaucratic decisions are sometimes subordinated to political decisions in a top-down fashion. Accordingly, there are many cases in which an individual would tend to decide on a certain policy. Obviously, there is not the degree of consensus-building that one finds in Japan. One side effect of this is that an individual bureaucrat in Korea will tend not to see lateral issues that other sections or individuals are working on as clearly as will his Japanese counterpart.

I mentioned earlier that the shift to knowledge-intensive industries requires experienced human resources. The current maturity of the human resources in Korean ministries could be characterized as very advanced intellectually but having much room for improvement in terms of actual experience. As in large Japanese firms, Japanese ministries take students right out of college and mold them into realistic bureaucrats. But Korean ministries recruit some of their people out of foreign—particularly American—universities, students who tend to have excellent ideas that many local Koreans would view as unrealistic. While rotation of personnel between various sections of a ministry takes place in both countries, the Japanese tend to maintain some human resources as specialists, particularly in bureaus that require high knowledge content, such as electronics. Generally, within MITI of Japan, I find that the bureaucrats are very well versed not only in technical understanding, but also in general awareness from historical to current events, and of course, in the massive data of their industry. It is this very possibility of give-and-take that gives Japanese bureaucrats the clout to make effective administrative guidance possible without the law. In Korea people are often rotated frequently through various bureaus and sections and, as an example, I once found a section chief I dealt with in the electronics-related department at the then Ministry of Commerce and Industry being replaced by a textile man from another section who spoke a totally different jargon. Again the issue of stability seems to distinguish the two countries.

In addition, the dynamics between the ministries and the diet are quite distinct. In Japan, where the diet is composed of elected members, some of the representatives have been reelected quite a few times and as a result have become fairly well versed in certain areas of specialization. Thus there is a cadre of representatives that are quite expert on, for example, the area of trade policy. In Korea, where a significant part of the diet was politically appointed, turnover was such that that type of know-how accumulation would not occur as smoothly and, as a result, informed debates between the representatives of the ministries and diet members based on expertise are seen less frequently in the arena of trade issues.

While the Korean system perhaps looks less mature and effective than its Japanese counterpart, it has one significant advantage. Part of the inertia of the Japanese trade policies—namely Japan's inability to respond quickly to the criticisms and actions of foreign trading partners—is a result of the consensus system that involves many bottom-up policy proposals. (This is partly the crux of what Wolferen describes in his *Foreign Affairs* article, "The Japan Problem.") Thus, for example, even if the Japanese prime minister decides that a certain type of action needs to be taken in order to appease foreign trade pressure, he may not be able to push that policy through. Rightly or wrongly, due to its top-down nature and composition, the Korean system can react fairly quickly to direction coming from the top layers of government. Of course, one would want to make sure that the direction is correct; however, in this regard, the fact that Korea can learn from Japan's successes and failures probably improves their hit rate in comparison to a situation requiring the navigation of uncharted waters.

ALL A MATTER OF TIMING AND THE ISSUE OF PREEMPTION

It is becoming increasingly clear that controlled economies whose influence on the international scene is nontrivial will be forced to liberalize. They really have no choice. The only residual question is the rate at which the transition from a controlled to a liberalized economy will occur.

As in corporate strategy, where the notion of sustainable competitive advantage is key, countries will try to position themselves in a favorable manner such that they can sustain their comparative advantages for the longest period possible. Since success breeds inertia, this tendency isn't hard to understand. But given the international interdependencies of many global industries, trading partners will simply not allow such an advantage to continue indefinitely.

Recently, a television documentary in Japan compared the economic development of two countries that were devastated at the end of World War II—Japan and Germany. It was clear from that program that Japan had a policy that could be partially summarized in terms of aggressive exports, controlled imports, maintaining the yen at as low a level as possible for export competitiveness, creating an environment in which labor hours continued to be excessive despite maturing of the economy, and self-sufficiency of parts and equipment.

The television program asserted that Germany, on the other hand, joined NATO and the EEC and liberalized import markets earlier, recognizing that domestic industry must compete with imports. Some German firms make it policy to try to buy parts for export products from markets to which the finished products are exported. When the French criticized Germany for working too hard, the Germans acceded by legislating certain mandatory vacations. The Germans today work about 800 hours less per year than the Japanese do, and they are still asking for more reductions. It is well known that European nations have a social welfare system that makes Asian nations look miserly. Professor Bruce Scott at the Harvard Business School has said that a country has two types of output—economic and social. As this television program illustrated, Japan had basically neglected social output in favor of economic output. Germany also appreciated its currency, the Deutsche mark, before it was forced to. The Japanese went to the brink, and fear struck as the "Nixon shock" took place in 1971. From an economic perspective, in 1961 Germany became the second largest GNP nation following the United States in the Western world; that position was overtaken by Japan in 1968. Yet there is no "Germany bashing."

Japan is possibly the richest country in the world financially, but it is also quite probably the only country in the world that is the object of criticism in terms of so-called Japan bashing. This is largely because requests by foreign nations to liberalize were only responded to when a crisis occurred.

For Korea, following the Japanese model is a reasonable strategy only so long as the model continues to work. However, given the state of Japanese international relationships today, Korea has several issues to worry about. First is the concept that strategists call preemption. The Japanese have said that it is sometimes better to be number two than number one because it takes much more overhead to become and maintain the leadership position. The bad aspect of being number two is that a strategy that worked for number one may not work for number two because it has been preempted by number one. Let's look at Korea as next in line to Japan in terms of economic development in the Far East. When one looks at the amount of time it took for the United States to react to some of the Japanese policy "excesses," there has been a considerable amount of delayed reaction. Yet, once the "giant woke up," the United States has been much more sensitive to the same policies being used by Korea. As a result Korea would naturally have much less time to sustain such a policy. Take, for example, the semiconductor industry. Only after the Japanese took over a 90 percent share of the 256K

DRAM (dynamic random access memory) marketplace in the United States did the U.S. government get really serious about the matter. Today, the Koreans have a single-digit market-share position in the U.S. marketplace and the U.S. is already saying that it ought to monitor this very carefully and ask the Koreans for voluntary export restraints. Number one got stopped after attaining a 90 percent market share; number two got warned at less than 5 percent. When one looks at this phenomenon, it is clear that Korea will not reach the height of Japanese economic output solely by following the Japanese economic strategy.

Secondly, it would perhaps behoove Korea to start acting like Germany in the manner mentioned earlier. And, to an extent, Korea is already doing so. As was the case in Japan, there are always people who are fearful of liberalizing too fast. And, recently, a prominent economist turned high-level bureaucrat was removed from office because he advocated liberalization of the domestic market too strongly. Yet Korea is slowly starting to appreciate the won. Korea is also trying to even out trading patterns as mentioned before by trying to import parts from the country to which it exports and by trying to change the destination of its exports from predominantly the United States to European and other nations. While Korea is clearly the record breaker in the newly industrializing economies (NIEs) with respect to hours worked per year, the rounds of worker protests that occurred in the summer of 1987 have slowly started to change these parameters. This, combined with the top-down structure of Korean government, would probably make Korea react faster to the pressures of trading partners compared to Japan's inertia. In any event, the timing of liberalization at this point is probably the most important hinge factor in Korea's trade strategy, and the cost of liberalizing too early or late would be phenomenal.

Despite the internal and external criticisms that abound, the Korean government has to be given fairly high marks for managing its economy as well as it has from a Korean standpoint. Was that selfish? Perhaps. And it sought tolerance particularly from its trading partners, citing that the country was still fragile and growing.

To the foreign businessperson, the Korean government has generally been helpful if the foreign concern was willing to contribute to the Korean economy in ways that the Korean government desired. Otherwise it was probably better for the foreign firm to not get involved with Korea. This is still the case, by and large; however, due to the issue of timing, liberalization of the economy is taking place at a rather fast rate, and each step taken in this direction represents change that almost always signifies an opportunity for the foreign businessperson.

3

Strengths and Weaknesses of the Korean Economy

The Han River runs majestically through the city of Seoul, hence the growth of the Korean economy is often referred to as the miracle on the Han. There is a lot of coverage of this "miracle"; however, my view is that, as in Japan, much is misunderstood about what is truly miraculous and what is not. A proper perspective on the economy is quite important, particularly when Korea is part of a corporate strategy or at the government level of public policy. The previous chapter considered some of the government policies that were put in place in Korea; this chapter seeks to illustrate through statistics some of the interim results. Because too many books present only statistics with observations that aren't logically connected, I have organized this chapter so that the statistics underlie salient messages intended to convey the key aspects of the economy.

On an absolute scale Korea is still small compared to the visibility it is getting. Korea is clearly not in the big leagues, yet it gets a disproportionate amount of press and attention. Publicity is a two-edged sword—the positive aspects are more opportunities as a result of enhanced awareness; the negative aspects are the prompting of caution and fear to a degree that exaggerates the facts. Let me illustrate.

The reader knows by now that every economic discussion must start with a look at the GNP. In 1987, the U.S. GNP was $4.5 trillion, Japan's around $2.7 trillion (a figure recently buoyed by the enormous appreciation of the yen), and Korea's was $119 billion. Thus, in comparison with Japan, the Korean economy was less than one order of magnitude smaller. On the basis of share of world GNP, Korea is not quite 1 percent. To add some historical perspective, in 1960, Japan's share of world GNP was 3 percent.

Let's look at the size of private-sector firms. Of the largest corporations in the three countries mentioned, IBM's revenues are somewhere around $55 billion; Toyota Motors', $52 billion, Matsushita's and Hitachi's, $38 billion each, and Nissan's, $33 billion. The Samsung Group recorded $20 billion, standing slightly ahead of Mitsubishi Heavy Industries. The Hyundai Group of Korea is also around that size. So goes the usual narrative.

But, in all fairness, that is not an apples-to-apples comparison. One should not compare Korean conglomerates with individual Japanese enterprises. Comparing entities in the two countries at the group level, the Sumitomo Group, for example, showed 18.9 trillion yen (approximately $145 billion) as their revenue in 1987. Counting their 24 core companies, the Mitsubishi Group is even larger at $176 billion. One can also perform an apples-to-apples comparison at the individual firm level by comparing the revenues of Mitsubishi Electric, for example, at $16 billion, to those of Samsung Electronics, at $3 billion.

But Korea has been growing at an enormous rate and is clearly still in the growth phase of its national life cycle. The GNP per capita for Korea in 1987 was $3,132. Considering that in 1962 the analogous figure was $87, one can see what phenomenal growth means. When one compares the annual growth rate of GNP over the recent past, one finds:

COMPOUNDED ANNUAL GROWTH RATE OF GNP

	1975–79 (%)	1980–84 (%)
United States	3.2	1.8
Japan	4.7	3.9
Korea	9.9	5.3

Korea's growth rate is far in excess of what any advanced nation could show. (It is also of interest that the growth rates of all three countries have declined into the 1980s.) The Samsung Group, for example, has grown about fourteenfold in ten years. Shipment figures in leading-edge industries show similar explosive growth.

Korea, like Japan, has been very successful in a number of focused product arenas. When one looks at Japan's export breakdown, it turns out that a couple of products, namely, automobiles, auto parts, videocassette recorders, TVs, radios, and computers constitute about 50 percent of the total figure and 7 percent of employment. They have not been successful across the board—service industries, with the notable exception of the financial sector, are a good example.

Korea has had marked success in a number of limited product areas, although the figures indicate that in most cases, even in those industries, Korea's output is significantly smaller than that of Japan. In the steel industry, where the Japanese talk a lot about the Korean catchup, Korea produced about 16 million metric tons in 1987, whereas Japan produced 105 million metric tons in 1985. In the automobile industry, Japan's output in 1985 was

7.6 million units; Korea produced 756,000 in 1987 and is hoping for 1.25 million by 1990. While Japan dwarfs Korea in these areas, the Korean figures are quite healthy with respect to their own stage of development and environment. One can begin to see some of this in the consumer electronics arena:

PRODUCTION FIGURES FOR THE FIRST SIX MONTHS OF 1986, IN THOUSANDS OF UNITS

	Japan	Korea
Black-and-white TVs	465	2,564
Color TVs	6,588	3,051
VCRs	16,658	1,392
Radios	4,174	1,615
Tape recorders	24,192	7,253

In these product areas, high growth has brought the fruits of Korean labor into Korean households:

PRODUCT OWNERSHIP, 1986, IN UNITS PER HUNDRED HOUSEHOLDS

	Japan	Korea
Color TVs	170	80
Refrigerators	110	80
Automobiles	81	5

Perhaps the biggest miracle is that Korea has accomplished this amount of growth under a very severe set of conditions—its "success" is still fragile. If Korea has achieved anywhere near the success that Japan achieved in the sixties—which it certainly has done in a number of product areas—and if Japanese growth has been called miraculous, Korea's development has to be one of the most amazing economic feats in history.

To start with, Korea is small. The U.S. population is around 240 million, Japan's is 120 million, and Korea's is 42 million. From a landmass standpoint, Japan spans 378,000 square kilometers as against Korea's about 100,000 square kilometers. Its dependence on foreign energy sources is about as bad as Japan's; there just aren't many natural resources in such a country. Korea's only outstanding asset is its people—probably the key force behind its success and a topic I will come back to.

Another constraint Korea faces, particularly in comparison with Japan, is in the area of finance and capital. It is a real wonder that Korea has been able to finance its growth. Vis-à-vis the Japanese economy, the Korean economy bears two major burdens in this respect. The first is defense spending. In order to maintain stability and sovereignty in the face of the enemy across the border, Korea is saddled with a sizable military force:

DEFENSE SPENDING: JAPAN VERSUS KOREA

	Percentage of GNP		Percentage of Government Budget	
	Japan	*Korea*	*Japan*	*Korea*
1975	0.8	4.4	6.2	28.8
1980	0.9	6.3	5.2	35.6
1985	0.99	5.2	6.0	30.6
1986	0.99	5.1	6.2	31.2

It is certainly one thing for a once-affluent country like the United States to be spending more than 6 percent of its GNP on defense; recently there has been more criticism in the United States that this isn't affordable in the face of large deficits. And since the Japanese government has relatively much more capital available to fund industrial projects, it has a lot more freedom with respect to financial support of strategic industries, particularly in the realm of research and development.

A financial handicap that in a way is self-inflicted is that Korean households save much less than their Japanese counterparts. It seems almost intuitive that a stable society tends to save relatively more: The savings are safe. Comparing the period 1982–86, American households saved about 8 percent of their disposable income; their Japanese counterparts saved about 18 percent; and Korean households about 9.6 percent. The Korean government reportedly wants to see this at about 13 percent in the near future.

Earnings from trade are, of course, the other source of funds. It is well known that Japan's trade surplus is huge. Korea has just managed to balance its books:

CURRENT BALANCE: JAPAN VS. KOREA, IN BILLIONS OF UNITS

	Japan	Korea
1984	$35.0	−$1.4
1985	49.2	−0.9
1986	85.9	4.6

Since Korea has been running current account deficits for some time, it obviously has to finance its growth from external debt. Japan is well known as a creditor nation—in fact, it has been criticized for lending Americans money to purchase Japanese products. Korea, on the other hand, is a significant debtor nation; its foreign debt in 1981 was $17 billion; by the mid-eighties that had grown to $45 billion. Continued deficits certainly build cumulative debt. In 1987, thanks to the 1986 surplus, Korea could reduce its outstanding debt to $36 billion. It is clear that

Korea needs to continue to run trade surpluses until it is comfortable that its foreign debt is under control.

To draw an analogy between countries and corporations, Korea is a corporation that is growing at perhaps the maximum possible rate, financing its growth largely from leverage that it hopes to service through its earnings. Everyone learns that the financial risk of such a strategy is much higher than that of a corporation that is financed by recycling its profits and equity—hence the point made earlier about fragility.

Interestingly, Korean private-sector firms are run according to exactly the same philosophy. I mentioned that the Samsung Group grew fourteen times over ten years. That is dramatic exponential growth. But let's look at some of the other indicators of that group. Its profitability during the past several years has been about 0.8 percent, and its debt-to-equity ratio about 3:1. One often talks about growth or market share versus profitability—and it's clear that the Koreans have chosen the former and perhaps gone even further than that by taking on significant leverage. In the United States such an operating philosophy is certainly not considered to be conservative.

Adding to this fragility is the fact that the Korean economy depends on exports to a much greater extent than does the Japanese economy. Korea exports about 36 percent of its output, whereas the comparable figure for Japan is about 16 percent. In this day and age of trade friction, one could say that, from a government standpoint, domestic business is more controllable than export business.

To underscore again this point of fragility, the Korea Development Institute, a government-related economic think tank, has done some sensitivity analysis of various scenarios. Particularly influential are the appreciation of the won and wage increases. A 10 percent appreciation in the won could apparently reduce GNP growth by 1 percent. A 5 to 6 percent increase in wages could significantly cut GNP growth as well (their aggressive growth target of 9.5 percent for 1987 was simulated to go down to 5.8 percent), and unemployment would be almost 1.5 times the pre-wage-increase levels. One could always question the assumptions underlying such a scenario; however, what is clear to me is that the Korean economy does not have the resiliency of the Japanese economy, which weathered a more-than-40-percent appreciation in the yen over a two-year period. For those who remember, in the early eighties when the dollar dropped to 178 yen, everyone (on both sides of the Pacific) was forecasting that Japanese enterprises wouldn't survive. As of this writing, the dollar is hovering in the 120-yen range, and Matsushita and several other firms have said that they have revamped their cost structure so that they could weather a lower-than-130-yen dollar.

It is literally amazing that Korea took such a risk and has so far been able to make ends meet. While at Harvard Business School, I remember reading a case about Sears, Roebuck and Montgomery Ward where Sears took the high-leverage position and made it work, grew, and expanded its market share relative to the financially conservative Montgomery Ward. In that particular situation, I'm fairly sure that even if Sears had been more financially conservative, while it might not have seen such phenomenal success, it would still have been a viable business. Korea is unfortunately in a situation where, if it didn't take the high-leverage route, it could not grow fast enough to kick itself out of less-developed status. And one must admit that compared to a whole host of other non-NIE Asian nations, Korea has done remarkably well.

SOME FACTORS UNDERLYING
KOREA'S SUCCESS

As alluded to earlier, first and foremost is basically the only resource that Korea has, and that is human resources.

The important factor to consider in this area is both the wage and what one gets for that wage—not solely the former factor.

Labor: But let's look at wages first. The following table compares wage levels by country:

WAGE LEVELS FOR SELECTED COUNTRIES

Country	1985	1987
Japan	$14,124	$22,458
Korea	3,590	4,224
Taiwan	3,593	5,290
Singapore	5,850	5,087
Hong Kong	3,460	3,460
Malaysia	1,560	1,560

What one gets for that wage is, first, a highly literate workforce. One couldn't do much better at 97.5 percent literacy rate. And second, that workforce is very industrious:

HOURS WORKED PER YEAR

Country	Regular Hours	Additional Hours	Total
U.S.	1,742	156	1,898
Japan	1,947	221	2,168
Korea	2,833	—	2,833

The Koreans, believe it or not, make the Japanese look lazy. Japanese businessmen used to work on Saturdays— many no longer do. The Japanese who are stationed in Korea are occasionally asked by their Korean business associates to meet on Sunday and transact business (not play golf). Most Japanese would give up a Saturday, perhaps, but not a Sunday. That is one sign of Japan facing maturity.

The year 1987 saw labor unrest in Korea. While such high industriousness at very low cost is good for the economy, it is obviously very stressful for the workers themselves. There are basically two reasons for this stress and unrest. First, the worker's family operates on a very tight budget and sometimes a deficit. A television program on the subject reported the example of the family of one worker in which the husband brings in about 260,000 won per month. The total family expenditure per month is 320,000 won. Taking into consideration fluctuation in the value of the won and using any number between 700 and 800 won to the dollar, and one will see that that isn't much to spend per month. And the family is still running a deficit, so the wife either has to work or the family must seek financial help from relatives. Second, there is much differentiation in wage rates depending on educational levels. A university graduate gets approximately three times what a high-school graduate gets. In addition, prior to 1987 there was no or little compensation for overtime and nominal fringe benefits compared to Japan. It seemed that in 1987, the unrest turned nationwide, and most enterprises settled for a 20 to 30 percent increase in wages.

It is interesting that this unrest occurred when it did. In 1987, too, Hyundai Motors agreed to recognize a company union representing the workers. I recently visited Toyota Motors and found out that their company union was established twenty-five years ago. Perhaps it's about time.

Korea also has room for improvement in terms of unemployment; the government is well aware of this. While every country measures unemployment in a different way, Japan's unemployment hovers between 2.5 and 3 percent, while Korea's hovers between 4 and 5 percent, Since Korea adopts the ILO (International Labor Organization) methodology of calculating unemployment rates, a person who works more than one hour per week is considered employed. Thus, relatively speaking, the Korean unemployment rates tend to be underestimated relative to comparable statistics from other countries. When one goes to Korea and asks around, one finds a lot of new graduates from second-rate universities having much trouble finding jobs. In addition to the work ethic, perhaps that is why the Koreans work so hard: One is lucky to have a job—better hold on to it.

Big-business orientation: It was mentioned that the Korean government followed the Japanese model of emphasizing scale in the design of its industrial policy. Not only is industrial concentration high in Korea, it gets more concentrated with time. That is to be expected since the bigger the base, the faster the growth on an absolute scale. Looking at the top ten conglomerates in Korea, in 1977 they were responsible for about half of Korea's GNP. In 1984 it only took the top five conglomerates to make up half of Korea's GNP. This trend can also be seen by looking at individual groups like the Samsung Group. In 1975, Samsung's revenue was about 3.7 percent of Korea's GNP; that figure had risen to 6.4 percent by 1980.

As the Japanese found out a long time ago, there are two basic problems with high industry concentration. When the top thirty groups, who do much more than half of the GNP and constitute over 70 percent of exports, employ only about a quarter of the labor pool, it becomes rather difficult to keep people employed. Japan developed a whole network of subcontractors, parts suppliers, wholesalers, distributors, and retailers around the big enterprises to try to alleviate this problem. They still want to nurture small business more aggressively. That movement is already in motion in Korea. Second, big firms become bureaucratic anywhere in the world, and some of the best creative products and services come from small-to-medium enterprises. The software industry is a good example of this. So some of Korea's thrust into high technology will depend on such smaller-scale endeavors. But by and large, in the product categories mentioned earlier as Korea's successes, capital intensity is one of the common characteristics, and one has to accept that scale is a very important factor.

Population growth: Korea has managed to keep its population growth under control. Many people underestimate the importance of this factor to economic development. It is closely related to the supply and demand for food, urban planning, infrastructural planning, and so on. Korea's year-to-year growth in population has been around 1.2 to 1.6 percent. I recall a government program in which, if the head of a household agreed to a vasectomy, that qualified the individual to receive very favorable financing on a home mortgage.

The inducement of foreign technology: The Japanese have acquired foreign technology at a very reasonable cost. They negotiated 42,000 technology contracts in the thirty-three years between 1951 and 1984, for $17 billion. This apparently represents around one-fifth of the current annual U.S. R & D expenditure for the United States. It is difficult to do a true apples-to-apples comparison, but the Koreans negotiated 3,500 technology contracts between 1962 and 1985 for $1.3 billion. It seems that the cost of this technology was about right, but in number of contracts negotiated, there is a lot of room for catch-up.

All in all, the Korean economy deserves very high marks despite the aspects open to criticism. And the Korean government seems to be very aware of the areas for improvement and has fairly effectively nudged industry in that direction. In relation to the stage of development Korean industry is in, many Korean economists were more than adequately trained in top United States institutions. And one cannot underestimate the advantage of having the benefit of hindsight through the Japanese experience.

KOREA VERSUS SOME OTHER NEWLY INDUSTRIALIZING ECONOMIES

One reason why Korea attracts more attention than its scale warrants is that as a group, the newly industrializing economies—Korea, Taiwan, Hong Kong, and Singapore—are starting to make a dent in market share in certain product categories. And Korea is the most visible in that crowd, particularly because of the publicity associated with the 1988 Olympics.

Take for example, production volumes in consumer electronics:

PRODUCTION VOLUMES, FIRST SIX MONTHS OF 1986, IN THOUSANDS OF UNITS

Product	Japan	Korea	Taiwan	Hong Kong	Singa-pore	Total NIEs
Black-and-white TVs	465	2,564	561	62	60	3,247
Color TVs	6,588	3,051	1,483	202	903	5,639
VCRs	16,658	1,392	167	—	—	1,559
Radios	4,174	1,615	5,172	19,901	587	27,275
Tape recorders	24,192	7,253	6,321	5,423	5,356	24,353

In this list, it is clear that the only category in which the NIEs as a whole haven't surpassed or come close to Japan is in VCRs. In fact, Japan's share of the world consumer electronics market has been going down. Again, compared to any one country, Japan is still dominant; but compared to the NIEs as a whole, Japan may have something to worry about. And Korea is the closest to Japan and most visible.

Let's look at the economic indicators of the four countries in 1985:

	Korea	Taiwan	Hong Kong	Singa-pore
GNP (in millions of dollars)	81,253	60,186	34,225	17,731
GNP per capita (in dollars)	2,032	2,868	6,311	6,519
GNP growth (percent, 1981–85)	7.5	6.5	5.8	6.0
Composition of GNP (percent)				
Agriculture, fisheries, steel	15.3	6.5	0.7	1.1
Manufactured goods	28.1	40.9	23.9	24.0
Construction	8.1	4.3	5.3	11.0
Trading, Finance	23.4	17.4	37.7	41.4
Other	25.1	30.9	32.9	22.5

A couple of things leap out from these statistics. First, Hong Kong and Singapore have considerably different characteristics from the other two countries, in that they are service economies to a much larger extent. Korea has the largest GNP, but the lowest per capita GNP, mainly because Korea has the largest population. Korea's population is more than double Taiwan's. To anyone who has been to Hong Kong and Singapore, it's quite obvious that while the population density is extremely high, the landmass area is so small that per capita GNP is boosted.

Korea also had the highest growth rate over the five years shown. The only way for Korea to achieve that was the leverage factor mentioned previously. Taiwan, a smaller-scale country from the population and area standpoints, exports more than Korea does in absolute dollars. Taiwan has run a surplus on its balance of trade since 1976, whereas Korea's deficit continued to run deeper until recent years, when the country has just been able to make ends meet. That is one of the reasons Taiwan is a net creditor nation while Korea is deep in debt.

Again, one aspect that helped Korea achieve this growth even with such high risk is concentration of big business. It is illustrative to look at a comparison with Taiwan and Hong Kong, for example, in electronics:

CONCENTRATION OF CAPITAL, ELECTRONICS INDUSTRY

	Number of Manufacturers	Market Share of Top 15
Korea	1,112	73%
Taiwan	2,632	21
Hong Kong	1,435	10

That's pretty dramatic. Again, in capital-intensive industries like automobiles and semiconductors, high capital concentration is a big advantage. Also, while employee turnover rates in large Korean firms are far in excess of their Japanese counterparts, they in turn are far lower than turnover rates in small-to-medium enterprises in either Korea or Taiwan. In some cases, such rates in smaller firms can reach 50 percent.

It is clear that within the NIE category, Korea and Taiwan are the closest rivals. There are many similarities, such as dependency on foreign components, major export markets, and export product categories. But there are many differences as well. They include Korea's "export or die" philosophy, which provided tight capital preferentially to the biggest exporters versus Taiwan's export policy, which was balanced by policies to stimulate domestic consumption of products. Also different is the role of the general trading firm in the two countries. In Taiwan such firms are usually independent firms; on the other hand, up to ten Korean trading firms were selected by the government for export, and these firms play a central role in the conglomerates of which they are a part.

From a financial perspective, the cost of capital has been rather different. Taiwan's prime rate has been hovering about 4 to 6 percent higher than that of Japan for the past decade and a half. The range of fluctuation of Japan's prime rate is about from 4 to 9 percent. Taiwan's range is from 11 percent to about 16 percent. And Korea's has fluctuated between 13 and 24 percent. Given this cost of capital disadvantage, the only way for Korea to compete in capital-intensive industries was to aim production at large export markets and provide preferential low-cost money to the most successful exporters. That made the rest of the economy pay even more for money.

From an exchange-rate standpoint, both Japan and Taiwan maintained a fixed exchange rate until 1971–72. Since then Japan's currency has appreciated nontrivially, and Taiwan's at a moderate rate. Korea's currency, the won, has been regulated by the government, and the result is a reverse U-curve over time. The won started at around 130 to the dollar in the early sixties and ever since then has depreciated, until a few years ago it reached a high of 890 to the dollar. Now it seems that both Taiwan and Korea are being pressured to appreciate their currencies— as of this writing, Korea was forecasting lower than 700 won to the dollar very soon. The potential for both currencies to appreciate is one factor that has made various U.S. and Japanese manufacturers consider moving their subcontracting activities to countries in Southeast Asia that are less prone to this type of pressure, at least for a while. Some prominent Western economists have advocated the view that Taiwan should appreciate its currency faster than Korea, in light of its better financial position. I wonder, though, whether Western governments will think with that level of detail when discussing trade policy.

There are many other interesting points of comparison among the newly industrializing nations, but an exhaustive analysis is beyond the scope of this book.

RELATIONSHIP WITH THE NORTH—
A PROBLEM UNIQUE TO KOREA

While South Korea lives in a very tough environment, perhaps the toughest of these problems is North Korea. This is very frustrating because it is so tragic, and it seems that there is very little that can be done about it. The reason I choose to discuss this problem in this chapter is that a good part of the problem is economic. Before we get to that, however, I need to fill in a little background.

Korea was formally annexed by Japan in 1910. Thirty-five years later, Japan surrendered to the United States, and Korea regained its status as an independent nation. Approximately two years would pass until the Soviet Union and the United States would gain administrative control over the northern and southern halves of Korea. At the time, the 38th Parallel was chosen to be the dividing line. That was the origin of the division of the country.

There was considerable confusion during the period beginning around 1947 until the end of the Korean War about what socialism in North Korea meant. While many were forced to go north, some chose to go north thinking that was utopia; many came south as well. In some families, there was a division of opinion as to which side individuals wanted to be on. The net result was countless numbers of divided families—that is, families in which some members live in North Korea and the rest in South Korea. They have been separated for over three decades without any means of communication with each other. Remember the emphasis that the Confucian influence places on the family. And then think about the realities of the situation with respect to the North. There is only one way to describe the image of several women who visit the river just south of the border and scream out *Omoni, Omoni* ("mother, mother") in the direction of the North Korean mountains, with no hope that they will ever be able to see their probably living mother. If that is not tragic, what is?

By all measures, the economy of North Korea is in a sorry state. As of the end of 1985, the South Korean GNP was 5.5 times the size of its northern counterpart. The South Korean economy is growing at twice the speed of that of the North. South Korea's trade volume is 20 times that of the North.

From an industrial standpoint, about the only item of which North Korea produces significantly more than the South is coal; they produce 60 percent more. The South produces 24 times as many automobiles, 14 times as many ships, and 46 times as many television sets.

Perhaps that isn't a fair comparison of two countries that have such different ideologies. Yet, by all accounts, the North Korean standard of living isn't even adequate. Just because a country is socialist doesn't mean that its citizens can starve and go without adequate clothing and housing. Recently a fairly well-educated North Korean doctor and his family defected to South Korea via Japan. Since he published a book, his account of North Korea is available to the general public. He mentions that he and his wife had never seen white rice until they left North Korea. His amazement at what he saw on arrival in Seoul is exemplified by his disbelief that the South produced most of the cars in the streets of Seoul. Apparently, food is rationed, and the rationing is so tightly, centrally controlled that people who don't believe in the official doctrines get their food supply curtailed. (This is probably an extreme form of the carrot and the stick. The People's Republic of China and German Democratic Republic aren't quite that bad.)

The extent to which North Korea is a closed society is second only to Albania. Perhaps it is good that North Korean citizens don't know what is going on on the other side of the border—if they did, much instability and unrest would ensue. Ignorance is bliss, after all. But apparently, while people in their late forties and fifties still have some doubts, the younger generation is completely brainwashed.

When I am in Japan, I find occasionally that members of North Korean organizations—not knowing which Korea I am from solely from my name—leave their newspapers in my mailbox. These newspapers state, for example, that the Korean War started when the "American empire" invaded North Korea. They were the victims. Now, I've read books about the Korean War that allege that perhaps the attack by the North Koreans wasn't a complete surprise—that intelligence had picked up signs in advance of abnormal circumstances. Yet the North Korean newspaper account, which the defector also confirmed was common knowledge in the North, seems to be a gross distortion of facts. Obviously there are countless examples of this sort of propaganda. They posit South Korea as an extension of the "American imperialist state," and all North Korean citizens vow aloud that they will banish from this earth every person that associates him- or herself with that state until the last drop of blood has drained from his or her own body.

To whom do they vow this? Of course, to Chairman Kim Il Sung, and his son Kim Jong Il. (Interestingly enough, they *have* seen white rice. What little there is of it goes to the "first" family and surrounding personnel. That's obviously what North Korean socialism is all about.) If the South is to be criticized for an autocratic regime and be seen as a target for Amnesty International, perhaps a look at the North is in order. The general view is that Chairman Kim is at least a stabler human being than his son, whose accession to power as heir apparent is feared. At Harvard I learned that the irrational competitor is much more to be feared than the brilliant, logical one.

What makes this something of a cause for alarm is that while the economic gap between the South and the North continues to widen, the North has made sure it doesn't fall behind in military strength. As mentioned previously, the South's GNP is five to six times the North's; from a standpoint of military spending as a proportion of GNP, the North spends four times as much as the South. The North Korean military forces stand 750,000 people strong as compared with 540,000 for the South plus about 30,000 U.S. military personnel stationed in South Korea. The North has about 750 fighter aircraft as compared with 360 in the South, plus an additional 100 contributed by the U.S. The South, however, has a larger navy—110,000 tons versus the North's 72,000 tons.

Juxtapose these four factors—divided families separated from relatives they cherish; a sorry economic state; a somewhat less-than-rational head of state who brainwashes his citizens not just with ideology but with blatant distortion of the facts, aiming to antagonize the South; and a reasonably strong military capability. That is called playing with fire, and it is involuntary. Even for the greatest of strategists, there is no easy solution to this problem, and the hope is that increased visibility in terms of trade, and other events like the 1988 Summer Olympics, will contribute to stability in the Korean peninsula.

I have tried in earnest to present to the reader the Korean economic situation, its strengths and problem spots, in an understandable way. While Korea clearly is still not in the big leagues, it is growing very fast and is fairly successful in a number of focused product areas. Labor and large-scale businesses are among the factors underlying Korea's success. A comparison of Korea and some other Asian newly industrializing economies showed its major competitor to be Taiwan. And North Korea was highlighted as a very difficult problem economically, politically, and militarily.

Korea has been relatively successful up to the present, but it has a long way to go, and the road ahead is as—or even more—challenging, with many obstacles to overcome.

4

Capabilities and Strategies of Large Private-Sector Firms

B ecause the Korean economy tends to be so centered around big business, it is likely that businesspeople from reputable foreign firms are going to wind up dealing with large Korean firms in one way or another. Thus it is quite important for foreign businesspeople to understand what big business is like in Korea, and where it is similar to or different from large Japanese businesses with which they are likely to have more experience.

SIMILARITIES WITH BIG BUSINESS IN JAPAN

It is perhaps natural that in some ways large Korean businesses look like their Japanese counterparts. After all, many of the top managers of these firms lived through the Japanese occupation. Moreover, during that era some of them yearned to and actually did study in such Japanese institutions as Waseda University, a school that even today is renowned in Japan.

The organizational factor: The first thing that the foreign businessperson recognizes on visiting a large Korean firm is that the office physically resembles its Japanese counterpart. Anyone who has been to a Japanese office knows how different that is from offices in American firms—close communication, maximal awareness of what's going on, lack of privacy, and so on. It can be argued fervently that such an office tends to promulgate a sense of community with close-knit communication and teamwork. From a more practical point of view, perhaps Japan and Korea have opted for this style because of the lack of real estate.

A deeper view of the Korean organization also gives the foreigner familiar with Japan a feeling of déjà vu. Individual employees belong to sections, sections belong to departments, and departments belong to divisions. Section managers are called *kwajang* and department managers are called *bujang,* which are precisely the same Chinese characters for *kacho* and *bucho* in Japanese, meaning the same thing. Usually, division managers or one level above—that is, director level, are officers of the corporation. Even the various grades of directorship, namely the managing director, *sangmu;* senior managing director, *junmu;* and vice president, *busajang,* are the same characters as their Japanese counterparts, *jyomu, senmu,* and *fukushacho.*

Various firms are also organized into business groups. The Samsung Group would be an example somewhat analogous to the Mitsubishi Group of Japan. A typical group might contain a trading firm, an electronics firm, a chemical firm, a construction firm, and so on.

I would caution the reader at this point that a more than cursory view shows some major differences deep below the surface, which I shall describe in a later section. But it is still the case that the overall similarity to Japan is probably the first impression that strikes the foreigner.

Diversification strategies: In the evolution of big business in both Japan and Korea, it is necessary to understand the evolution of their product lines over a period of time. Diversification is a fairly well-studied phenomenon, and firms diversify for a number of reasons. They diversify because, from a strategic standpoint, if they don't their product might be replaced by another new technology or idea. They diversify because growth in their original product line has stopped, and they think that their capabilities can be better mobilized in another field. They diversify because industrial policy provides incentives for businesses to diversify in a certain direction that is deemed to be in the national interest. (This is obviously not meant to be an exhaustive list; there are many other reasons as well.)

When one looks at the product evolution of the Samsung Group, it entered into sugar and wool textiles in the fifties; fertilizer, paper, and electronics in the sixties; synthetic textiles, electronic components, petrochemicals, heavy industry, shipbuilding, and construction in the seventies; and semiconductors, bioengineering, and aircraft in the eighties. One notices first that the product line evolved with the development of the Korean economy as a whole— that is, simple products in the fifties, the start of the building of a social infrastructure in the sixties, the emphasis on know-how intensive products in the seventies, and a high-technology focus in the eighties. Some of this shifting was clearly motivated by the government through positive incentives such as preferential financing. The goal was to seek consistency between public and private-sector strategies so that the development path would go from light industrial goods to heavy industrial goods to knowledge-intensive products. This is precisely the same as in Japan.

This does not mean, however, that all Korean business groups diversified in precisely the same manner. The Lucky Goldstar Group entered the chemicals field in the late forties; electronics in the late fifties; energy, steel, and construction in the late sixties; and so on. It is quite evident that there are some basic differences between the two groups, particularly in their choice of what businesses to enter and in their timing of entry. While the basic industrial trend from simple to complex products is visible here as well, the timing of entry, particularly into electronics, is rather interesting—this will be considered in greater detail later.

Government motivation to the private sector can be negative as well as positive. It may be well known that Japan's MITI once had a plan for the auto industry based on the idea that competitiveness in the small-car product segment required scale, and that in order to maximize this effect there should only be one manufacturer of small automobiles. Everyone knows that this plan was never accepted by industry; there are seven or eight manufacturers of small cars in Japan today.

Clearly the Korean government also had a heavy influence in the domestic automobile industry there. In fact, for a while there was only one manufacturer of the lower-end automobile (cars with engine capacities of about 1,500 cc or less)—Hyundai Motors. Today Hyundai is well known even in the United States through the success of their export model, the Excel. It is interesting to note that this business is missing in Samsung's product lineup. Industry analysts have said that this is a case in which—despite the group's desires to enter this business—the government and the company could not agree on the method and timing of entry.

The story of how Hyundai entered the shipbuilding business is particularly interesting. Chairman Chung of this group apparently felt that the capabilities required to build ships were quite similar to those required to effect construction projects. It could be argued that this is an example of capability-based diversification; that is, deploying resources that one already has toward an area with a related set of capabilities. A Japanese example of this would be Nikon and Canon diversifying from the camera business to the semiconductor lithography equipment business, since they were both based on optical technology.

However, what is particularly interesting in the Hyundai example is that the chairman reputedly turned in the lowest bid to an overseas customer as a first attempt before he understood what it took to build a ship. This seems to be a case of "get the order first and figure out how to do it later"—yet, from a results standpoint, he did make a viable business out of this thought process. This is also reminiscent of certain consumer electronics firms in Japan that issued binding quotes to U.S. manufacturers for sub-contract manufacturing before the Japanese firm even built a factory and knew what their costs were actually going to be.

It may be natural that these similarities exist particularly when, for example, the late Chairman Lee of Samsung used to spend a month every year in Japan studying what new products and technologies had been introduced in the past year.

Technology acquisition from abroad: It is hard to imagine that just three decades ago both Japan and Korea had little industrial know-how. The quickest way to fill that gap was to cooperate with foreign firms. The government also aided this process by only allowing foreign firms that were willing to transfer know-how to participate in the domestic marketplace—through foreign exchange controls, for example.

As the statistics in chapter 3 show, outside procurement of technology is a very efficient process compared to internal generation of technology. The Mitsubishi Group of Japan, for example, has been involved in countless numbers of partnerships. Chrysler and Mitsubishi Motors have cooperated in the manufacture of automobiles. Westinghouse and Mitsubishi Heavy Industries, and also Mitsubishi Electric, have cooperated in the heavy electronics arena. Caterpillar and Mitsubishi Heavy Industries have a long-standing joint-venture relationship in industrial vehicles.

The Koreans have also been quite aggressive in this arena. In the automobile industry, for example, Hyundai has a rather close relationship with Mitsubishi Motor and Mitsubishi Corporation (trading). In 1973 technology for producing the 1.2 liter engine was transferred to Hyundai from Mitsubishi. The two Mitsubishi firms are both 7.5 percent investors in Hyundai Motors as well.

Daewoo, which acquired Saehan—the company that was originally positioned in the segment above subcompacts (between 1,500 and 1,999 cc)—cooperates with General Motors of the United States and is now aggressively pursuing the subcompact category. General Motors is a 50 percent investor in Daewoo Motors. Kia Motors, another aggressive competitor in the subcompact category, is trying a rather interesting approach—a three-country joint venture that includes Mazda (8 percent), C. Itoh (2 percent), and Ford Motor Company (10 percent). It is also well known that the Ford Motor Company is a minority investor in Toyo Kogyo, otherwise known as Mazda. Samsung and Chrysler tried to cooperate in the arena of automotive parts, however, this apparently did not materialize. Clearly, the alliances are forming fast. All of them are exporting or planning to export to the United States market—it will be interesting to see how the U.S. automobile market structure will evolve.

The Koreans are clearly not at the Japanese level in automotive technology. However, it can be argued that the catch-up is occurring quite fast. For example, it was in the late fifties that Nissan first exported their Datsun model 210 to the United States. The Japanese went through a long period of product, technology, and manufacturing improvements until their cars made significant headway into the U.S. marketplace in the 1970s. The Hyundai Motor Company, as mentioned before, acquired 1.2-liter engine technology from Mitsubishi in 1973 and exported their first Hyundai Excel to the United States in 1985. By 1987 it had become an astounding success.

It is interesting that many of the major automotive alliances are joint ventures, not straight licensing arrangements. This must have come about for a variety of reasons, but I recall once talking to a high-level bureaucrat in the Ministry of Trade and Industry who said that the joint venture allows the Korean firm continually to upgrade the technology, whereas straight licensing makes the transfer of successive new technologies subject to situational factors to a much greater extent.

Export orientation: Following the guidance provided by the government to focus on exports, big business in Korea does significant business in export markets, as does Japanese business. The only difference is that since the Japanese domestic economy has also matured, the domestic marketplace occupies a much bigger portion of sales relative to Korean firms, whose export markets are much larger than their domestic market.

The strategies that the Koreans have used to penetrate the U.S. market bear remarkable resemblance to those used by the Japanese. They first exported products as subcontractors for major U.S. manufacturers and retail outlets, perhaps even sold nonbrand merchandise, and then finally embarked on sales with their own brand. Their distribution strategies start from their own trading house offices based in the United States, and once they embark on sales with their own brand, they first try to sign up second-tier distributors and retail outlets—with the main objective of initially maximizing the number of pipes to various geographic regions in the United States—and then they upgrade the distribution channels, perhaps to first-tier distributors. In terms of advertising and PR, they, like the Japanese, have hired U.S. agencies and executives so that the messages look very American. A few years ago, I even noticed that Samsung was promoting its own brand of color TV as a prize on a U.S. television game show. Samsung has also put up a huge sign in Times Square. In addition, they have arranged for various service and maintenance networks, which often become the hinge factor when a consumer considers purchasing a product. Perhaps the Koreans have something of an advantage in the hiring of executives for their U.S. subsidiaries. If they are able to attract executives with experience in U.S. subsidiaries of Japanese firms, they not only learn about how the Japanese have done it, but also run much less risk in terms of adapting already internationally experienced personnel to their subsidiaries.

Emphasis on manufacturing: In the early phases of Japanese and Korean industrial development, there is no doubt that manufacturing was the key function that provided them the advantage—not design or sales. Their strategy is clearly what Michael Porter of Harvard Business School would call "cost leadership," allowing them to start from the low end of the marketplace and work themselves into higher-niche markets.

The mind-set that underlies this emphasis seems to be the same whether in Japan or Korea. The key to low cost is good quality (so as to minimize rework or service costs), procurement of quality parts at the lowest possible cost, low labor costs, low capital costs, exploitation of the learning curve by following it all the way to maturity, exploitation of the concept of scale so that overhead is spread thinly on a per-unit basis, shrewd utilization of manufacturing equipment, and the "do it right the first time" philosophy. The driving force behind this whole strategy is the much-talked-about market-share orientation. Thus, in a way, manufacturing drives marketing. I find that many U.S. firms have a totally different philosophy. Often, either product strategies or marketing strategies drive manufacturing, with profit being the concern over market share.

The only difference is that the Japanese do it a lot better today. The only advantage that Korea has is lower direct and overhead labor costs, and in some cases costs of capital. The Japanese cost-reduction philosophy is quite impressive—they have weathered a 50 percent cut in the value of the dollar in just over two years (1985–87). An equivalent slide in the won-dollar exchange rate would propel Korea into a crisis. Another example would be Korean products that are successfully marketed in Japan. Koreans introduce products in Japan at fully 25 to 30 percent less than the Japanese counterpart products, based mainly on the factors mentioned above. The Japanese have tried to match pricing, for example, in the case of videotapes, and later try to make up for the differential in labor costs through shrewder procurement of parts and perhaps more modern manufacturing technology.

A number of years ago, there was much debate about whether it was smarter for Japanese firms to move their production to lower-labor-cost countries or to automate and reduce labor content. The trade-off is obviously between labor costs saved and increased equipment depreciation of the additional automation. I have seen a number of these so-called lights-out factories in Japan and, clearly, they are much more advanced than the best factory I saw in Korea. Yet, there is a limit to how cost-effective one can become by using automation. And, in fact, some Japanese firms say that that is not the primary reason for automation.

What I have observed is first, that unless considerable thought has been given to the design of a flexible automation system, automation results in much less flexibility and consequently less ability to spread overhead across a variety of different product lines. Secondly, the labor–cost depreciation trade-off only works in favor of cost reduction when the line utilization is high. And last, the Koreans are not avoiding automation either—they are moving in that direction. Thus, when the dollar dipped below 150 yen, Japanese firms rushed to Korean and other newly industrializing economies for lower-cost manufacturing.

Perhaps the factor that attests the most to the similarity in manufacturing emphasis is summed up in a comment that I heard from a Japanese executive. It used to be that the Japanese considered manufacturing know-how to be very valuable and not to be seen by foreign eyes. Recently, however, I have noticed that they have loosened up about this, particularly with respect to Westerners. According to the executive, he has shown his factory to quite a few Americans, in some cases competitors, who ask unlimited numbers of questions and take copious notes. Almost invariably, however, the impact this has had on manufacturing competitiveness back in the States turns out to be minimal, because the bits and pieces they pick up in the Japanese factory are not transplantable given the American management culture, philosophy, and system.

However, the Japanese are still very sensitive toward letting Koreans into their factories, because much of the setup of Korean factories was designed using the Japanese as role models, with know-how transferred through technology, equipment vendors, individuals, and so on. When the Koreans pick up a hint from a Japanese factory, they can apply it almost immediately.

There are probably a lot of other similarities in how big business functions in Japan and Korea. There is a considerable advantage to the fact that the Koreans have a target in the form of Japanese achievement, whether it be market-share position, production quantity, cost position, and so on. And the philosophy has always been, "get there, but get there a lot faster." Some of the similarities mentioned here are more than superficial; however, when one looks below the surface, there are a lot of differences between the private sectors of the two countries.

DIFFERENCES FROM BIG BUSINESS IN JAPAN

In business, everyone wants to think of themselves as being different from others. This is particularly true of the Japanese and the Koreans. Each country tries to differentiate itself from the other, and much of this is emotional. However, occasionally, one runs across some comments that seem to be logically correct, giving rise to meaningful differences.

Maturity: Korean big business is generally much younger than its Japanese counterparts. The Samsung Group was founded in 1938. The Mitsubishi Group was founded in 1870. The symptoms of being less mature, perhaps even an adolescent, make themselves evident in a number of arenas. The first is obviously size. As mentioned before, the Mitsubishi Group is perhaps twenty times larger than the Samsung Group, and the individual companies are significantly larger as well. Anyone who has been in management knows that with this degree of size difference, organizational systems would differ significantly in maturity.

The first of these is separation of ownership and management. The well-established groups in Japan no longer have the founder's family members actively involved in the management of the group or any of its member companies. The only large firms in which the founders are involved are obviously the fairly young ones—examples are Sony, Honda, Casio, and Matsushita. I mentioned earlier that the family is a very important element in Confucianism, and that Korea and Japan had ascribed different levels of importance to this. In the old days the large Japanese groups tried to carry on the founding family's tradition, but today when one looks at these four companies, Honda particularly has a very pragmatic attitude about managerial succession. In fact, not only is there not even a hint of nepotism, but each president has been particularly careful to retire voluntarily and to transfer management when the slightest sign of a slowdown in his abilities manifests itself.

Korean big businesses are quite family-driven. The Samsung Group has the famous Lee family; the Lucky Goldstar

Group, the famous Koo and Huh families; and the Hyundai Group, the famous Chung family. Family members still have significant holdings of the group shares. And two of these groups have gone through a full managerial transition—the Lucky Goldstar Group and the Samsung Group, whose founder recently died. The current chairman of the Lucky Goldstar Group, Koo Cha Kyung, is the son of the founder. Just to illustrate, the vice chairman in charge of the electronics business at Goldstar is the chairman's brother and, reporting to him, the head of the computer and communications division is yet another younger brother of the chairman. Yet, all in all, the Lucky Goldstar group has gone through a fairly smooth transition—no doubt due to the harmony (*inhwa*) that is a central cultural value.

The other two groups are still strongly dominated by the philosophies of their founders. In 1987, both men were in their seventies and were legendary figures. They also tended to be the key decision makers with respect to any significant partnerships with foreign firms. As a result of worries about the prospect of an unexpected transition, both chairmen announced their transition plans in early 1987. In the case of the Samsung Group, the chairman's third son took over the top job on the founder's death. In the Hyundai Group, the brother of the founder is now "operating chairman," so to speak, with founder Chung Ju Yung as "honorary chairman."

Ever since the end of World War II, when the *zaibatsus* were broken up, the Japanese groups have not had strong centralized management. This is perhaps another measure of maturity. For example, the Mitsubishi Group has a super-management committee made up of the presidents of the twenty-eight core companies and called *Kinyo-kai* ("the Friday committee," because that's the day they meet). They may make decisions that affect the entire group, such as the group entering into an entirely new business. However, this committee doesn't even go into the operations of a troubled member company and try to improve the situation.

By contrast, the Samsung Group has something called the chairman's office. This office is in charge of the group's planning and administration, and also serves as a watchdog for poor performance. What distinguishes this office from, say, the *Kinyo-kai* of the Mitsubishi Group and the Mitsubishi Research Institute, which collects much industry information for planning and consulting purposes, is that a group called the implementation committee of the chairman's office at Samsung will actually descend upon a poorly performing member company if corrective action submitted by that member company's president doesn't produce results. The committee is like a paratrooper and will investigate and audit to the point where a better corrective action plan could be written and executed. Sometimes, this could lead to the firing of a president. This is reminiscent of Harold Geneen's management style at ITT, where good performers are left alone and ruthless intervention is used with poor performers. A Japanese group would seek to improve performance by intervening at the company level, not the group level.

Some organizational differences: As one can see above, Korean firms tend to be top-down driven and, despite the individuality of the people, execute such direction. The key aspect that contributes to this operating style is the fact that Korea is a military state. There is a world of difference between the young generation of Japan, who are starting to take on rather liberalized values, and the young of Korea, who are still mandated to serve three years of military training. These three years condition Korean youth to take top-down direction, develop endurance and persistence, and work as precisely as one can as a team.

Some Korean firms take advantage of this and design their new-hire training to include somewhat militaristic exercises, such as having to hike a couple of days through mountains, and so on. Even in Japan, some companies do this—perhaps not quite to this degree—but compared to employees of companies that don't do such things, the employees seem to complain a lot less about little inconveniences.

The other aspect of military training is awareness of the enemy. In this regard it is easy for South Korea to think of North Korea as its military enemy and Japan as its economic competitor. This is perhaps why such intense effort exists to catch up with Japan.

Human resources: Large Japanese firms have tried to practice permanent employment. Recently, this system has started to deteriorate; however, it is clear that such a system had numerous merits. Large Japanese firms have a cadre of managers very experienced in the business and, also importantly, in getting horizontal tasks—that is, tasks that require coordination between various different functions—accomplished. Japanese firms rotate their employees, and most do not make it to management until they are at least in their late thirties. A Japanese *kacho* (section manager) usually has about fifteen years of experience, and a *bucho* usually has more than two decades of experience. As mentioned before, the Japanese are more "village" oriented than the Koreans are, in that they will share their fate with an organization like a company. While both would say that the family comes first, the Koreans practice that principle much more vigorously. This is why turnover is so much lower in large Japanese firms.

In contrast, despite their good intentions, Korean firms do not practice permanent employment. This is true from both directions. Namely, when a manager performs poorly, he can be let go. What a Japanese firm tries to do is either find a way to make him improve or assign him to a different job—in other words, it is the company's responsibility if a person doesn't perform right in a job despite his best effort.

From the other end of the spectrum, the Korean employee can also quit and switch jobs. In Japan, the cost of switching companies, particularly between large firms that do not practice lateral hiring, is infinite. The stigma attached to a quitter in Japan is that that person had a flaw, and the responsibility of not being able to conform to a particular company or organization's culture is placed squarely on the employee's shoulders. Thus, even when the company invests significantly in training the employee with advanced know-how, the chances are that he or she will not take off with that knowledge.

Not so in Korea. Recently, I was talking to someone in the software industry there, and he was continuously mentioning how, as soon as an employee has enough know-how to make him more valuable than what he is paid, he takes off for another firm. More income is not only good for the individual but also good for his family as well. Most Korean firms have turnover percentages in the teens, whereas Japanese firms have turnover rates in the low single digits. I was quite astounded to hear recently that a director-level executive of a company in a major group in Korea quit, went as a director to a direct competitor—another large company—and after three months came back to the original company. This type of move is simply inconceivable in the large Japanese company environment. Thus, the retention rate of know-how within the organization is much lower in Korean than in Japanese firms.

The good side of this phenomenon is that the Korean organization is much more tolerant with respect to heterogeneity. They take people from other firms, from abroad, and they move people around fairly freely. After having lived in Japan for over a decade, I am convinced that the Japanese are genuinely afraid of heterogeneity. As a result they tend to become rather inbred and tend not to take the initiative in a large number of cases. The Koreans are much more open than this not because they tried to, but because their country has had heterogeneity forced on it for so long. During the Korean War, for example, the ROK (Republic of Korea) forces had to fight hand-in-hand with the UN forces. There is no room for being particular about homogeneity. I will discuss the benefits of this in the next chapter, in which the phenomenon of repatriating foreign resident Koreans will be touched upon.

Competition and cooperation: Large Japanese companies and firms are fairly open about cooperation with multiple partners who can potentially compete with one another. For example, one trading company may use one subsidiary to cooperate with one U.S. firm, and another subsidiary to cooperate with a direct competitor of that U.S. firm. Of course, the U.S. firm usually prefers not to engage in such a situation.

Also, the relationships between large Japanese firms, even if they are competitors, is very interesting indeed. For example, company A in Japan could be company B's competitor, yet be buying components from company B, and could be a contract manufacturer for another product line. In each case, however, the purchaser is very careful that he doesn't compromise his purchasing power through such arrangements. Thus, Japanese firms rarely take sides naively.

While there is some of this in Korea as well—that is, one occasionally hears of Samsung buying components from Goldstar, for example—by and large quite an esprit de corps tends to be built around a particular group. Of course, there are human ties at the individual level, such as coming from the same university or industrywide projects organized by the government. But the general rule seems to be to compete among Korean firms, and cooperate and compete with foreign firms. Japanese firms practice cooperation and competition with both domestic and foreign firms. This is another difference between the Koreans and the Japanese that makes the Koreans slightly more comfortable to deal with for the American businessperson—who tends to have a strong desire for a partner to remain "pure."

UNIQUE KOREAN SKILLS

Having compared some of the characteristics between large Japanese and Korean firms, it would be useful to understand what the Koreans do distinctly well vis-à-vis the Japanese or Americans. Many of these are the skills that have helped the Koreans achieve the success that they have enjoyed so far.

Negotiating from a position of weakness: Even in the West, many scholars have studied a phenomenon called the power of the weak negotiating party. Korea, I would say, has been a master at this, and I credit both the private and the public sectors for this. Traditional wisdom says that in a negotiation, the side that has the least of value to give will wind up with a bad final position. Empirically this is not always the case. The Koreans, for example, have walked into countless negotiations with little of apparent value and, in the end, came out with a good deal.

Numerous factors combine to make this happen. When I was a student at the Harvard Business School, I once encountered a situation called a coalition game. Let us call the three players A, B, and C. There are four settlement possibilities—AB, BC, AC, and ABC each having a different settlement payoff. In a two-way settlement, the two players negotiate how the payoff will be shared, and the remaining player is left empty-handed. The game is usually set up so that one of the players, say player C, ends up having the least to offer, and as such begins the game feeling that he or she is going to be cut out.

First, there is the emotional factor. What was found after many threesomes played this game was that when the three people played the game through a computer terminal—that is, so the players didn't know who the other players were—what was expected happened. Namely, the two strong players cut out the third player and maximized their payoffs. But, negotiations in real life rarely happen in this manner. In a more realistic case, where the negotiation happened face to face, the weakest party almost always stayed in (I think it was more than 90 percent of the time). Most of us have a real problem leveraging a weak party right in front of our eyes.

Second, it was surprising to note that in the situation where one party was, in fact, cut out, the player who was in the middle power position (not the strongest, not the weakest) ended up getting cut much more often than one predicted at the outset. The strongest party is obviously leveraging its power to search for the best deal there is. The weakest party, fearing that it is likely to end up empty-handed, tends to try to give the strongest party an even better deal than the player with the middle power position by cutting its own returns; that's certainly better than ending up empty-handed. The middle player, particularly in a situation where the dealings between the other two players are not known, tends to underestimate the payoff that the weakest player is offering to the strongest. In the real world, I have seen many variations on this fundamental concept, in which a Korean firm, a Japanese firm, and an American firm in the same industry are trying to form partnerships, all trying to leverage the other parties. Often the Korean firm is perceived to be in the weakest negotiating position, and the American firm is perceived to be at the other extreme. I have seen this phenomenon quite a few times.

What reinforces this is pure negotiating skill. One should not forget at the outset that the Koreans are very serious when they negotiate—it is a matter of executing well the very limited number of options available to them, and the cost is often survival. They will know or learn by rote to use every negotiating skill there is. Slow and infrequent concession patterns are almost a way of life in Korea, if only because they are so poor and their resources so limited. Companies from more affluent countries tend to yield here. The Koreans also know exceedingly well the value of information in a negotiation and will spare no effort to get critical information.

As was the case with Japan over a decade ago, when a Korean firm makes a deal with a foreign firm (Japanese or American), the government used to intervene not only to prevent foreign exchange and antitrust violations but to advise the firm when it was overpaying for technology or accepting terms and conditions that are too restrictive. While the Korean government is shifting toward the negative-list system that only scrutinizes deals on an exceptional basis, this checks-and-balances system provided additional incentive for Korean firms to get a reasonable deal from foreign firms. And, Korean laws were often reinforcing in this regard.

Ability to turn change to one's favor: Still vivid in my impression is the soccer game between the Koreans and the Japanese that decided who was going to participate in the World Cup. These games are always quite emotionally charged—no doubt due to rivalry that stems from some historical differences. The result was that the Koreans won. I frankly did not know who to root for, having fairly close emotional attachments to both countries, but I was particularly fascinated by an observation by the commentator for that match. He said that the Japanese team had a very thorough game plan, and that as long as the game was turning out according to that scenario, the Japanese had the upper hand. And indeed they did. He added, however, that the Koreans would never give up under any circumstance trying to usurp the ball from the Japanese almost to the point where it was annoying to the observer and, in fact, when there was disarray in the game and the ball became free (like a fumble in football), the ball almost always ended up in the "hands" of the Koreans.

This, I thought, was a piercing observation, particularly in view of the contrast between the Japanese preference for stability and the Korean familiarity with turmoil that was mentioned in the first chapter.

At Harvard one of my professors said that luck is inevitable in business, and that some who may not appear to be so bright or experienced will get ahead because of luck. But he added that in the long term, being successful in business requires that one be positioned to leverage luck when it strikes. The Koreans have been quite good at this. When the so-called three lows (the price of oil, won, and interest rates) struck, Korean firms were charged up to rake in the business. And they did, as can be seen from the enormous growth rate they got during this period.

Being positioned for luck requires that one have an organization that can shift directions and execute very rapidly. Large Japanese firms and some American firms have either become so bureaucratic or so consensus-driven that they watch as opportunity passes them by. The Koreans have two characteristics that make them distinct in this regard. The first is the phenomenon described in the soccer analogy. The second is the military orientation that was mentioned previously. A sudden about-face even when carried out well produces tremendous stress in the organization, but for now the Koreans are hungry enough to put up with this.

Korea is also very effective when it comes to projects that require a concentration of effort. Imagine a situation in which one asked for a certain product to be manufactured and delivered in six months. When this date was negotiated, it was fairly clear that this was already quite an aggressive schedule. Let's say that there were special circumstances and the customer had to have product within four months. The Koreans will find a way to "brute force" it, whether it be getting people to work around the clock in short spurts or bringing in additional labor in order to accelerate tasks not on the critical path. While Korean labor is clearly asserting its rights, in comparison with Japan or the United States—where labor regulations and practices do not even allow such degrees of freedom—Korea feels like the place where anything is possible.

Remember the previously mentioned example of the Kyeong-Bu Expressway that was built faster than the expectations of any non-Korean construction company? How about the four subway systems in Seoul that were put in place all at once? The Japanese may call that reckless execution. In fact, in all their haste, the Korean subway designers posted the station signs (which also indicate what the next station is) in a place that is practically invisible from inside the train. Nevertheless, the project was expeditious. The Koreans say that because they are coming from behind, if they took the same amount of time the Japanese did, they'd never catch up.

Upon cursory observation, the large Korean and Japanese enterprises look fairly similar. We mentioned similarities in organization, diversification strategies, overseas technology acquisition, export orientation, and emphasis in manufacturing. The similarities do not continue below the surface, however. Some of the differences have to do with maturity of the enterprise, motivation, human resources, and the trade-off between competition and cooperation.

In order to deal effectively with the Korean firm, it is of paramount importance that the Westerner understand precisely where the similarities and the differences are. It will be interesting to see how the similarities and contrasts mentioned are applied to a particular industry. In that light, the next chapter will delve further into the electronics industry as an example.

5

The High-Tech Push into Electronics

Korea has been making headway into the electronics industry as well as such traditional industries as steel, shipbuilding, construction, and automobiles. Somewhat like Japan, which made the transition from capital-intensive to knowledge-intensive industries—thinking that the latter were better suited to a country without many natural resources—Korea has put a lot of emphasis into consumer electronics (with reasonable success) and lately into the semiconductor and computer arenas.

Although the first commercial transistor radio was produced in Korea in 1958, it was only in the late sixties that the government started focusing on the electronics industry, particularly its export potential. The government's concern was made clear in 1969, when the Electronics Industry Promotion Law was enacted. Among other things, the law required routine formulation of an electronics sector plan by the Ministry of Commerce and Industry (now the Ministry of Trade and Industry), registration of all participants in that industry, establishment of a promotions fund for the industry, promotion of overseas investment, and the formation of industry complexes.

Since then the Korean electronics industry has seen explosive growth. In the mid-sixties, the industry's income was about $10 million; by 1987, it had grown a thousand-fold to $10 billion. Throughout the seventies production grew 44 percent per year and exports grew 53 percent per year.

To understand this thrust, one has to touch first on the notion of the strategic industry. One must say at the outset that in the West, there is considerable debate over whether this concept of industry targeting is effective or not. Japan has had quite a decent batting average in this regard, but its failures have certainly not gone unnoticed. The Koreans have, in this sense as well, the benefit of hindsight from looking at the Japanese experience. Thus, originally, the Koreans adopted the notion of strategic industry from Japan. The view in the Korean government was that during a country's development, the existence of industries on which private- and public-sector policy could focus is often advantageous, since such a focus could aid in keeping the industrial mix consistent with shifts in comparative advantage. For example, in the past, Korea has through its economic plans endeavored to emphasize capital-intensive industries when light industries were still the majority of industrial output. It was also claimed that this focus provided a method of allocating public-sector investment to areas of importance. Let's start looking at how Korea targets industries by first understanding how the choice of industry is made.

Selection criteria: Korea has traditionally emphasized export potential, but the concept of a strategic industry has recently become greatly expanded, as the following pages show.

1. *Export potential:* Products in the industry must have a track record of export success, implying that the

country's comparative advantage is being utilized. The prospects for additional development of international competitiveness are then examined. As an example, skill intensity would be consistent with Korea's labor advantages, particularly in view of the desire for the nation to secure high employment levels.

Export potential would, needless to say, include an estimation that world demand for that category of products is large and on a steep growth curve.

2. *Prospects for domestic demand:* Because of the heavy dependence Korea has placed on exports, the industry must make a significant contribution to increasing economic growth through consumption in the home marketplace—which has been called "the second engine of growth." Additional benefits will accrue if the demand characteristics for the products are income-elastic: The more the country develops, the more demand there is for those products.

3. *Advancement of the nation as a whole:* Korea's desire to join the ranks of advanced states is clear, and the industry must contribute significantly to that end. The fifth five-year plan explicitly positioned science and technology as a necessity in the country's development. Thus, not only is skill intensity required; knowledge intensity in terms of intellectual skills is essential in order to provide competitive R&D capability.

4. *Minimization of raw material dependency and potential for adding high amounts of value:* Korea's lack of natural resources would imply selection of products that minimize excessive raw material imports. Being able to add much value is key in two respects. First, it allows maximal earnings potential. Second, the industry would have the potential to develop specialized niches so that various competitors could coexist.

5. *Minimization of trade friction:* A head-on collision with an advanced nation in terms of competition would not be favorable; therefore prospects for intraindustry specialization would help international coexis-

tence. This would be an important criterion particularly if the industry has the potential of becoming
global.

6. *Beneficial side effects:* Desirable spillovers into other
industries are looked at. If the industry concerned
could, for example, add to the productivity of manufacturing in other industry sectors, this could have
sizable leverage.

The electronics industry as a candidate: This industry clearly
has reaped the benefits of Korea's past labor advantages.
It may be possible to continue progress by shifting attention
to productivity and quality. The high literacy rate of the
Korean populace vouches for a fairly high probability of
a successful transition.

Changes in employment composition bear out the contribution electronics makes to the advancement of a nation
as a whole. For example, U.S. Department of Commerce
statistics indicate that knowledge-intensive industries ac-
counted for 18 percent of U.S. employment in 1920; the
figure had grown to 46 percent by 1980. The Japanese
figures are analogous, but the transition occurred much
more quickly: Employment in knowledge-intensive industries in the early eighties was around 40 percent. Most
of the growth occurred since the late sixties.

A look at the Japanese experience with electronics suggests what some of the indirect benefits of pursuing that
industry would be. MITI of Japan has said that progress
has been spurred in such fields as data processing, scientific
engineering calculations, management science, industrial
control, and information systems. These disciplines, needless to say, are key to a wide variety of industries.

A look at the demand prospects for the industry would
indicate that the market size, growth, and income-elasticity
requirements are met. And as for the potential for value
added, a simplistic indicator would be realizable price per
kilogram exported. Perhaps this is a somewhat naive way

to look at value added, but one could see that electronics would win against steel hands down: The indicator for advanced electronics is two orders of magnitude that of steel.

Now that it is clear that the Korean electronics industry is a shoe-in, let us continue to further our understanding of it. A look at the composition of production is key. In the early eighties, for example, consumer electronics represented 42 percent of industry production, components 45 percent, and industrial electronics 13 percent. Industrial electronics would include such important product categories as computers and robotics controllers. This arena was underdeveloped compared to advanced nations: Japan touted 34 percent and the U.S. 77 percent. The components figure is reasonably high, but only because foreign companies wanted to do their component subassemblies in Korea owing to obvious labor-cost advantages. Thus, technology-intensive components such as LSI (large-scale integration) semiconductors are a very small part of that figure. If one categorizes the manufacturing of electronics products into two phases—a technology-intensive (perhaps fabrication) and a labor-intensive phase (perhaps assembly)—it is clear that, in the past, the interests of Korean firms seeking to increase exports and foreign firms seeking to take advantage of low-cost labor intersected in assembly operations. Thus the industry concentrated on assembly, and to that extent didn't focus on developing the technology-intensive phase of manufacturing. This, quite surely, also has something to do with the fact that fabrication, for example, would require far more technology transfer, something foreign firms would be less inclined to do.

This situation was suboptimal and even dangerous for Korea. A simple continuation of this strategy would have just about guaranteed that Korea's electronics industry would be substituted away by countries who had yet lower labor costs.

Three firms basically dominated the scene in the consumer electronics category. Prior to the early seventies, Korean manufacturers weren't globally competitive in this category; exports were only 20 to 30 percent of production. At that stage, these firms took products that were mature in the advanced nations and tried imitating them through joint ventures. It was in the seventies that consumer electronics exports started to grow significantly.

In the eighties, an electronics sector plan was formulated to provide even greater momentum to the industry. It contained many aspects that made it much more than a simple export plan. It addressed the problems previously described by examining such issues as domestic-technology development, technical-information acquisition from abroad, human resources development, and domestic market development. Back when the plan was formulated, production was expected to reach $13.2 billion by 1986, which we now know was a bit on the aggressive side. In addition, correction in the compositional distortion discussed earlier was planned so that by the early nineties industrial electronics would constitute approximately a third of total electronics production.

There are four reasons why this shift toward industrial electronics is almost mandatory. First, industrial electronics goods have the potential for much higher value added and, therefore, margin. An executive in a major Korean consumer electronics firm, for example, complained that just before the shift to color TV production started, they were making a margin of a mere 10 to 20 cents on each black-and-white TV set they exported. Second, industrial electronics offers much more freedom in competition. Many product market combinations can be targeted for positioning, and if necessary, intraindustry specialization could have a beneficial effect on trade friction. Third, growth in the industrial electronics category was and is projected to be the greatest. Even today, large Japanese consumer electronics firms are trying earnestly to diversify into industrial electronics such as the personal computer market. And last, the leverage that can result in benefits to other industries is greatest in the industrial arena.

The shift to industrial electronics, however, is easier said than done. Looking at the experience of advanced nations, one would have to say that this transition could easily span two decades or more. Thus the Koreans are starting with two product categories: LSI semiconductor devices (products that are the "brain and memory" of computer systems; these components are much higher density and have many more features than do the discrete semiconductors that were exported by Korean firms prior to the eighties) and microcomputers (personal and home computers). Although LSIs are technically components, and microcomputers could be construed as similar to a consumer product, success in these categories is crucial in the transition to industrial electronics. As we shall see later, semiconductors are a strategic building block to many end products in the industrial electronics arena. It is also well-known that the personal computer is key in the sense that it represents low-end entry to the information processing customer—who tends to migrate upward. These two product arenas also represent logical projections of products that Korean firms manufactured in the past, discrete semiconductors and consumer appliances. It is certainly a bit easier when one can make analogies. And, not to forget, the world demand for these products has been growing phenomenally despite cyclicality.

Technology acquisition: It was mentioned in the previous chapter that partnering was a key strategy when it came to accelerating the learning process required to catch up to the state-of-the-art. Of course, companies in advanced nations don't want the Koreans to attain state-of-the-art technology, particularly through their own help, as that would be setting up a competitor. However, even now, the gap between the Korean technological level and that of advanced nations is so large that there seem to be an abundance of mature products to license and have subcontracted. Moreover, the life of some of these products is so short that there is a continuous supply of generations of technology to be licensed without divulging the state of the art.

I would use the term *superaggressive* to describe such technology acquisition endeavors simply because Korea has done so much in this area. Take, for instance, the Lucky Goldstar Group. Goldstar Cable is a partnership with Hitachi, Goldstar Tele-Electric with Siemens of Germany, Goldstar Electric with NEC, Goldstar Instrument and Electric with Fuji Electric, Goldstar Semiconductor with AT&T, Goldstar Alps with Alps Electric of Japan, Goldstar Honeywell with Honeywell, and Shinyeong Elevator with Mitsubishi Electric. And in the consumer arena, according to a Japanese newspaper, Goldstar Company supplies radiocassettes to Hitachi and black-and-white TVs to NEC. Also, Goldstar has licensed air conditioner and refrigerator technology from Matsushita, and electric range technology from Mitsubishi Electric.

Looking at the Samsung Group, Samsung Electronic Devices is a partnership with NEC and Sumitomo; Samsung Corning with Corning of the United States for the manufacture of television tubes, for example; Samsung HP with HP of the United States, a partnership involving the HP3000 minicomputer product line; and Samsung GE with General Electric of the United States, a partnership involving medical systems. This list is certainly not exhaustive. That is proliferation all right!

Official partnering is, of course, the most visible method of technology acquisition. Other methods, too, are worth noting. Korean firms can access technology through purchase of manufacturing equipment from Japanese vendors, who often will train Korean customers as they do their Japanese customers, with examples from Japanese users. Another method is to have the Japanese company that designed a plant for a major Japanese manufacturer subtly replicate the design for a Korean facility. There is certainly a lot of know-how transfer here, too. And at the individual level, the *Wall Street Journal* recently reported that there seems to be an abundance of greedy, unethical Japanese who when offered more than their Japanese bonuses are very willing to help Korean firms with the know-how of their Japanese employers. According to a Japanese newspaper, one Japanese employer became so irate about this that the passports of its engineering employees were confiscated by the personnel department, to be used only on loan.

It was mentioned in conjunction with the five-year Electronics Sector Plan that tapping into Korean residents living abroad who work for American technology-intensive firms is another method of going up the learning curve. There were generally said to be two ways to reverse brain drain—first, have Korean firms put up R&D labs in the United States so that Korean residents in the United States can continue to live there while contributing to Korean society. And secondly repatriate key U.S. resident Koreans to Korea through various enticements. For example, in the semiconductor industry, there was such an endeavor. The repatriation packages were enormous: Often they offered at least the U.S. salaries plus various benefits that allow these people to live extravagantly in Korea. This is certainly an example of the "do it fast" approach that motivated Korean firms to acquire know-how in the form of people, ready-made technology, companies, and so on. While the Japanese do some of this, they tend to import know-how and then modify and develop it within their organization in a way that is tailored to their way of doing things.

Specifically, the significant aspect of this repatriation story is that the foreign residents came back into rather high-level positions within those corporations. These were people that were close to technological know-how in U.S. firms and had worked in U.S. firms for a number of years.

The logic behind bringing in such people is clear—it is often said that if one wants an advanced but deterministic task done, one puts some bright people with advanced know-how at the helm of the organization and has the lower levels of the organization execute by their leadership. The people that took these high-level jobs did so because in these positions they felt that they would be contributing significantly to their country and because directing a Korean operation from a senior level is a lot easier than trying as a foreigner to manage a relatively divergent set of Americans in the United States. Out of those heralded, there are a few examples where the individual has already left the Korean firm. While the rest have stayed, the issue of real interest is whether a large Japanese firm would have done something like it even in dire need of technology. Somehow I doubt it. Permanent employment and the seniority system in Japan create a delicately homogeneous organization. Bringing in ex-U.S.-resident Japanese as managing directors, particularly with compensation that allows them to live like kings, would seriously have disrupted the Japanese organization. Yet the Korean logic was that they were behind in semiconductors, and as a result, they had no choice but to take action like this to leapfrog the learning process. This is an important example of the Korean system being flexible enough to adjust in order to fill a critical need. While the Koreans are tradition-bound like the Japanese, they seem to become pragmatic and do some extreme things when the requirement is there.

Consumer electronics: It has often been said of the Japanese system that the domestic market weeds out the weaker competitors, and only the survivors export. The experience in the Korean consumer electronics market is interesting from this standpoint. When diversification of Korean conglomerates was discussed before, the astute reader will have noticed that Goldstar entered the consumer electronics business much earlier than Samsung, a surprising latecomer. At the time Goldstar had a commanding share of the domestic consumer electronics marketplace and seemingly impenetrable distribution channels. It is well known that Samsung today is the domestic market share leader in consumer electronics.

According to a former Samsung electronics executive who oversaw most of this era, they had to do something different in order to have even a chance of succeeding. Their scheme was first to build a factory complex that could leverage scale better than any existing factory of any competitor. In addition, they tried to add more value than their competitors by tying up with foreign firms that had know-how related to production of parts. In the case of televisions, Samsung Corning allowed them to manufacture picture tubes in-house, which was of advantage over those that purchased the part. Of course, penetrating the somewhat-established distribution channels was not easy, but by a combination of offering differentiated products, aggressive pricing, and by initially prospecting those distributors that were not pleased with their present supplier, they were able step by step to form their own channels. Soon overseas OEM deals even increased their asset turns further. Now, Samsung sells consumer appliances under their own label in the United States. And, so does Goldstar.

The only other worthwhile competitor in this arena is Daewoo. We mentioned expedient entry into a business; Daewoo entered this business by acquiring the consumer electronics business from the Taehan Group. Their share position is significantly lower than either Goldstar or Samsung, and one does not see many Daewoo-label appliances in the United States.

Until recently many of the products that Korean manufacturers produced were what the Japanese produced one or more generations before. But now Korean manufacturers are starting to become somewhat creative as well. In Japan, for example, Samsung successfully marketed a new product then unavailable in Japan, called the read-only videocassette recorder (a VCR that doesn't record) for about sixty dollars less than the least expensive full-functioning VCR. It turned out that there was quite a market for this—for those who only play rented tapes, for those who dub many tapes, and so on. Once this happened, the Japanese found themselves in the interesting position of trying to catch up by introducing an improved version of the read-only VCR. And the Japanese are watching as Samsung tries to market its already announced 4 mm videocamera and -cassette. Some Japanese manufacturers are skeptical.

The Koreans have successfully made the transition from black-and-white TVs, to color TVs, to VCRs. They export approximately two million VCRs into the United States; this is likely to grow significantly year to year. Anyone familiar with the consumer electronics scene in Korea would know that the one significant Achilles heel that these manufacturers have is that a significant part of their final product content is Japanese. For example, in a VCR, close to 70 percent of the parts come from Japan. Open a Korean VCR, and one finds Matsushita, Toshiba, and other brands.

Originally the Koreans were afraid that the Japanese would limit their market share by constraining the supply of components to the Koreans. They urged local content to lessen this dependency. Yet it turned out in many cases that the division of the Japanese firm that sells the component is different from the division that produces competing consumer appliances, and that the two divisions were autonomously run. As a result, the components division of the Japanese firm was often out to maximize its components revenues by selling as much as they could to Korean manufacturers.

There are two true weaknesses of depending on the Japanese so significantly for components. The first is trade and exchange rates. The Koreans in 1986 ran a $7 billion surplus with the United States in electronics, and a $6 billion deficit with Japan. Moreover, when the Japanese yen appreciated against the U.S. dollar, the Koreans should have been in a position to reap the full 40 percent shift, since the Korean won stayed fairly linked to the U.S. dollar. Yet, of course, on 70 percent of the content, which comes from Japan, the components costs actually went up in won, and thus only part of the gain is realizable.

A more serious weakness has to do with the fact that more and more of the advancement in consumer electronics technology is occurring at the component level. Take, for instance, the VCR. Japanese manufacturers are constantly improving the servomotor mechanism that controls the motion of the tape. They have recently been experimenting with integrating the algorithm for the start-up and wind-down of the servomotor into a large-scale integration logic component. Of course, in due time, this component would become available to the Koreans as well. However, this means that while the Koreans may be able to advance themselves in product-definition capability, in terms of technology they will never be able to surpass the Japanese until they can start integrating state-of-the-art consumer electronics technology into silicon.

This is an example of why the Koreans have become so serious about getting into the already competitive semiconductor business. There is a limit to the advancements one can make in the end product unless one has the components capability. Unfortunately, this is easier said than done, as the Japanese product life cycle for the component and the end product is no longer than nine months at the maximum, and thus catching up at the so-called application-specific integrated-circuit level is basically like trying to jump onto a moving train.

Semiconductors: The Koreans, as mentioned before, had been in the discrete component business for a long time. However, they became serious about entering the large-scale integration semiconductor chip business starting in 1979 and into the early eighties, for the reason I have partially described. I wish to delve into a discussion of the Korean semiconductor industry, since this illustration will provide an example of the Korean thrust into a highly controversial technology-intensive arena in more than a cursory manner.

It is an easy thing to say that one is going to enter the semiconductor business; it is quite another to actually do so at such a late date. The metallic oxide semiconductor technology (now the mainstream process technology for the manufacture of chips) was developed by several Western firms in the 1960s. The Japanese followed this Western advancement very carefully, and by 1972 some Japanese firms had licensed the technology and were on their way to manufacturing chips based on that technology. In this business the entry costs become higher every year; entering the business with a manufacturing plant cost a couple of million dollars in the late sixties, and today a fabrication plant costs on the order of $150 million to start up. Even the Japanese, who started late relative to the Americans, allegedly ran red ink until the 1976–77 time-frame when the MITI-guided VLSI project catapulted the Japanese manufacturers into a commanding position in the dynamic-memory marketplace. What makes this even worse is that starting in 1983, the industry plunged into an excess-capacity situation, which first made the business severely price-competitive and second, introduced a high level of political influence into the industry. Korean manufacturers began to realize that if they didn't enter the business in a hurry, they would never make it.

The other significant barrier to entry into this business is intellectual property. The Americans and the Japanese entered the business at a fairly early date; companies from both countries held patents on various critical technologies for the manufacture of an integrated circuit. And many have patent cross-licenses. Not so for the new kid on the block, since there aren't many patents to trade. As a result, if one licenses the technology from the innovators, as one must, one ends up paying fairly stiff royalties to numerous firms. Combined, these would add significantly to the cost structure of the Korean final products. Thus, newcomers have to be prepared not only for substantial investment in the face of substantial red ink for a prolonged period of time, but also an outflow of royalty payments that lessens whatever labor cost advantage they have.

That notwithstanding, three Korean manufacturers—Samsung, Goldstar, and Hyundai—entered the business with iron determination. While all three of these firms bundled the semiconductor business in the same organization with other electronics businesses so as not to show excessive red ink from an actuarial standpoint, they all started up the MOS (metallic oxide semiconductor) business with subtle differences. Samsung bundled its semiconductor business with its telecommunications business in one of its group companies, Samsung Semiconductor and Telecommunications (SST). They also formed a development center and pilot operation in Silicon Valley which was called Tristar, and is now called SSI, Samsung Semiconductor Incorporated. Goldstar started its MOS semiconductor operation in a joint venture with AT&T that was named Goldstar Semiconductor. This operation combined the semiconductor, computer, and telecommunications product lines. They also put up an office in the Sunnyvale, California, area. Hyundai took its semiconductor operation and wrapped it with the computer, printed-circuit-board assembly, and factory-automation businesses and incorporated it as Hyundai Electronics Industries (HEI). Their original plan was to establish and run a sister operation in Silicon Valley called Modern Electrosystems Incorporated, MEI, which would mirror the operations of HEI.

Each of these firms took a similar strategy in terms of its formation of leadership. Samsung brought in as its president of SST a man by the name of Kang Jin Ku, who is a seasoned veteran in the electronics business in

Korea, having started and grown the consumer business of Samsung from nothing to a commanding share position. They selected as his number two man Lee Sang Joon, a U.S. repatriate. He eventually wound up running their operation in Silicon Valley. Goldstar Semiconductor used to be run by Koo Cha Too, a brother of Chairman Koo of the Lucky Goldstar Group; assisted by two people, Pyung June Min, an ex-IBMer; and Kim Chang Soo, an ex-DEC (Digital Equipment Corp.) semiconductor technologist. Hyundai Electronics was run by the fifth son of Chairman Chung of the Hyundai Group assisted initially by Mike Bae, an ex-Xerox manager; and by Chun Dong Woo, an ex-HP semiconductor engineer. In each case, one can see that the top of the organization is either a member of "the family" or a seasoned veteran in the group, while they aggressively bring in the "imported managers" described earlier in order to tap their technical and managerial expertise.

Each of these firms also aggressively partnered in order to accelerate the technology learning curve. Samsung obtained its consumer component technology from Sharp of Japan. From a MOS standpoint, they bought out the 64K DRAM (dynamic random access memory) design and process technology from Micron Technology of Idaho. And, they partnered with Intel Corporation in a number of semiconductor-related product lines.

Goldstar Semiconductor, by the same token, obtained its original DRAM technology from its joint-venture partner AT&T. From a logic standpoint, they licensed Zilog's Z80 microprocessor, and Advanced Micro Devices' product lines. The combination of the imported managers and technology transfers undoubtedly accelerated the learning curve.

Samsung, for example, continued to invest quite heavily in its manufacturing capacity while trying to close orders with large original equipment manufacturers in the United States. They succeeded in getting IBM and others to qualify and use their DRAMs. Like most semiconductor manufacturers in Japan and Korea, they cut back on their capacity plans during the severe recession in 1985. At the same time, they aggressively built up their distribution channels by signing up as many distributors as possible to increase their coverage. And most of this marketing effort was spearheaded by a U.S.-based marketing organization located within SSI in Silicon Valley. It was quite clear that Samsung concentrated its initial overseas efforts in the U.S. marketplace. In Japan they worked through the Tokyo branch of Samsung Trading Company with little staffing. They also tried to sign up multiple distributors, succeeding moderately; however, there has already been at least one distributor who decided to back out. Generally speaking, in the United States, as long as the pricing is aggressive and quality is acceptable, most major customers will try using a newcomer's product to a significant extent. Not so in Japan, where some major electronics houses share this philosophy but others distrust Korean quality so much that they will simply not consider the possibility. From these two respects—that is, the distribution channel and customer purchasing preferences—it is clear that the U.S. marketplace is a far easier one than the Japanese, and thus trade drifts to the path of least resistance.

When comparing this series of actions with that of the evolution of the Japanese semiconductor industry, one again notes some similarities and differences. The primary difference is that of timing. The Japanese first entered the integrated circuit business around 1972 and competed in an also-ran fashion until around 1979–80, when the fruits of the government-led VLSI project catapulted the Japanese into a dominant position in the DRAM design and process technologies. They were so successful in this business that they became the technology leaders in this product category from the 1-megabit DRAM to (now) the 4-megabit DRAM (not yet commercialized, but practically developed). And at the 256K DRAM level, they captured approximately 85 to 92 percent of the U.S. market.

The Koreans seriously entered the MOS device business

in the early eighties with the 64K DRAM generation of products. The business had already become very competitive, with some of the toughest competitors being large Japanese companies. It was a bit like jumping onto a fast-moving train. The Koreans have been attracting a lot of attention because they are moving up the technology curve rather fast. Three Korean firms have already introduced DRAMs at the 1-megabit level and are forecasting that at the next generation, namely 4 megabits, they will be able to announce commercial production at the same time the Japanese do. In fact, several Korean manufacturers have banded together to perform joint research at the 4-megabit level, with government direction somewhat akin to the Japanese VLSI project.

Yet, from a scale and market-share standpoint, Korea is still minuscule. Its market share in both the United States and Japan is still in the single digits, even though Korean firms have been rather successful in signing up distributors and major customers. At the same time, the U.S. government is keeping a close eye on them in order to prevent another serious conflict like the one that led to the U.S.–Japan semiconductor agreement. The Koreans, however, have been gaining market share rather quickly, due particularly to the fact that a floor has been established for the pricing of Japanese-made DRAMs as a result of this agreement. And the Koreans have quickly capitalized on this imperfection, combined with the high yen. Nevertheless, as mentioned before, number one got to 90 percent market share before the red flag went up; number two is already raising flags at less than 10 percent market share. That is the cost of preemption.

Another effect of shorter history in the industry is one that relates to operational strengths. The Japanese certainly imported design, process, and manufacturing technology from Western firms; however, they have learned to evolve that technology breathtakingly fast on their own. From an R&D standpoint, the Koreans have either imported technology or learned technology through industrious reverse engineering of foreign goods. This they have done very well. However, in order to pursue original technology, large Korean firms have recently set up central research laboratories like, for example, Hitachi's.

From a manufacturing standpoint, the Koreans are still far behind the Japanese. In fact, labor cost and depreciation expenditures are the only aspects where they have a competitive advantage. Make no mistake, they have been able to grow and develop considerably from such competitive advantages. However, to sustain this growth, and to protect themselves from wage increases and competition from other developing nations, they need to consider many other sources of competitive advantage. From purely manufacturing-expertise standpoints such as productivity enhancement, quality control, inventory management, throughput time management, automation, employee education systems, and worker management, they have a long way to go. Again, these are arenas in which the Japanese may have got started by listening to Deming or Juran, who preached quality management starting in the 1950s, but since then they have evolved incrementally on their own. The establishment of such a continual self-improvement effort, which took the Japanese quite a bit of time, will also take the Koreans some time.

The problem of transplanting and evolving manufacturing technology is indeed an interesting one. Roger Bohn of the Harvard Business School talks about an interesting concept called static versus dynamic knowledge. In my experience the reason American firms have been largely unsuccessful in transplanting Japanese manufacturing technology is that they take static knowledge—for example, a snapshot of how a plant operates in Japan—and try to transplant it into a management culture that is totally different. In the case of Korea, the static transplant works to a certain degree because the infrastructure was set up to be similar to the Japanese plant. Yet they are far from understanding the dynamic knowledge that the Japanese have developed over a period of time. An analogy is modifying someone else's software program to fit one's own needs. The usual advice is to write one's own code, since it takes just as much time to understand another person's code enough to modify it. The original author of the code, on the other hand, can modify it at will because he or she understands the causalities involved. Korean industry must get to the point where it accumulates manufacturing knowledge like the original author of the software program.

Another reason why this step is not as prone to acceleration as some of the other arenas in which the Koreans have shown accomplishment in an amazingly short period of time is that these improvements require something that Professors Robert Hayes and Steven Wheelwright of Harvard and Stanford, respectively, call horizontal tasks. These are tasks—like productivity enhancement or quality management—that involve tight coupling between different functions. There is clearly a shortage of acceptable human resources to meet these demands, and when it comes to well-qualified candidates, the shortages becomes particularly acute. When visiting Japanese factories I am continually impressed by how knowledgeable workers or engineers are not only about their own jobs, but also about the manufacturing process in general. In Korean factories, by contrast, it is rather evident that the workers know what they are told to do but need to understand far more to contribute significantly to accomplishing horizontal tasks. When dynamic knowledge is accumulated at the worker level in Korean plants, we will indeed be able to say that state-of-the-art manufacturing technology is close at hand. Yet one could make an argument that the cultural profile of the Japanese organization tends to reinforce the strengths of accomplishing horizontal tasks and that the Korean culture is not so aligned. However, one should never predict limitations in performance based on such areas for improvement since there could be an innovative solution to these issues.

Another arena in which the Koreans will have to "jump onto a moving train" is customized products. The Japanese have shifted their design and manufacturing capabilities drastically to serve such multifaceted needs. Consumers today have so much information available to them that more than ever they are able to shop around for the product or service that best fits their needs. This is true in automobiles, semiconductors, consumer goods packaging, and so on. Serving these needs requires a radically new set of capabilities.

First, in order to develop such products, one must be located close to the customer. When the bulk of one's customers are in the United States, thousands of miles away, the only way would be to establish development capability locally. Doing that, however, would detach development and manufacturing, a step that often causes difficulties in coordination. Also, design needs to become far more automated than it is currently since customization requires that the turnaround time after an order is taken be minimal. This capability would certainly turn into a basis of competition.

Second, manufacturing in Japan is taking a very different form to service this need. The whole concept of flexible manufacturing (quite a departure from the mass production with which we are all familiar) is a significant challenge as one must handle a small volume and many-line-items type of manufacturing flow. In contrast, mass production used to mean a high volume and a small number of line items. Implementing such a system requires substantial know-how that includes software for shop floor control, unique material handling systems, and customized equipment. Korea is far behind in this arena primarily because it did not need to foster such capability, based on its competitive advantage in mass production. However, as other developing countries catch up, Korea will be pushed into these highcr-value-added arenas, and adjustment will be needed. Again, these capabilities are very expertise-intensive, and developing the appropriate human resources will be a process that cannot be short-circuited.

ISSUES THAT NEED TO BE RECKONED WITH FOR CONTINUED SUCCESS IN HIGH-TECHNOLOGY ARENAS

Protectionism: Even Korean government–related personnel are divided with respect to this subject. Those who support free trade advocate a rather aggressive liberalization of the economy rather than a delayed reaction of trying to preserve the current state. Some even go so far as to recommend Hong Kong's free market approach instead of the Japanese "band of protectionism" approach. Such an opening up would accelerate technology diffusion.

Those who don't quite believe in being so progressive have suggested other means of minimizing trade friction: (1) local content in the form of setting up foreign subsidiaries, (2) diversification of export markets, and (3) product differentiation and segmentation such that head-on collisions would be avoided.

These responses fall into the category of being "easier said than done." Local content would surely have a diminishing effect on the very competitive advantage Korea touts—labor costs. Diversification of export markets is a difficult challenge, as any businessperson who has built up distribution channels would know. And when one is far away from the market one serves, it is quite difficult to find unique niches; that is probably one of the reasons why "going after the low end" has been most successful for the Japanese and Korean producers in the Western markets.

Brain drain: Although there are some remarkable repatriation stories, the number of technologically capable Koreans who opt to live abroad is still high. Reasons include national security, differentials in standard of living, education for their children, and the relatively individualistic culture of the Koreans compared with the Japanese. Many of these second-generation Koreans living abroad are inaccessible to Korean firms. It is really a challenge when one doesn't have enough good people to begin with and, at the same time, one can't hold on to the few that are good.

Relatively small domestic market: Korea's population is about one-third that of Japan. Therefore its domestic market also tends to be significantly smaller.

A small domestic market has two basic disadvantages. The first has to do with innovation. While Americans are thought to be creative, the innovations in the United States have as much to do with the fact that the enormous demand mandates producers to continually innovate as it has to do with the "creative" culture of the American people. "Necessity is the mother of invention" goes the saying. Up until now, the Korean process of taking foreign designs/ products and adapting them for domestic use has worked. In the future, if Korea is seriously to endeavor to catch up to advanced nations, it needs to define products in its home base and adapt them for export markets.

The second disadvantage has to do with hindering international competitiveness. It is often said that Japanese firms compete aggressively in the domestic market, and the winners export on a worldwide basis. In other words, the domestic market is a weeding ground for poor performers. I'm not sure this is true anymore even with respect to Japan when looking at companies like Sony, but certainly this option is not as available in Korea, where the market is significantly smaller. At the same time, if one sells considerably in the domestic market, then not only does one reap benefits in terms of scale and learning, but also one can consider selling export units at incremental pricing if one has progressed significantly toward break-even volumes on that product. Of course, one runs the risk of being accused of "dumping," depending on how it is defined.

Tight capital and high capital costs: We have mentioned the tight financial situation that Korea is in, caused by large government expenditures and preferential credit allocations. Many high-technology product lines are capital-intensive, and thus high capital costs would have a negative effect on the cost structure. The low cost of capital that the Japanese enjoy is certainly a competitive advantage in the world marketplace.

Preferential credit allocations used to allow major exporters in strategic industries to get around this. However, Korea is under external and internal pressure to liberalize its financial markets. This would suggest that such favoritism could slowly go away.

Intervention caused by political and other exogenous factors: Sometimes the political power base is mobilized in such a manner that certain industry decisions are affected in a seemingly arbitrary manner. There were a number of situations where strong personal connections to a high-level member of the government resulted in decisions that either delayed or jeopardized technological progress for the sake of a small minority. Recently the government has been on the move to diminish such favoritism. It will take a while to put an end to these unofficial influences, but it seems that improvement *is* taking place.

Government involvement compared with Japan's: The first difference is that in the old days when exchange rates were fixed, Japan could use balance-of-payment deficits caused by high growth as an excuse for direct financial support of an industry. Ever since flexible exchange rates were introduced and the electronics industry in Japan became competitive, Japan has been criticized by its trading partners to the effect that such subsidization was unfair. For Korea this point will come much earlier because Japan has already raised the world's sensitivity to such government support.

Second, industrial policy in Japan is administered through MITI's informally providing "industry vision" and what is called "administrative guidance." This means that MITI officials who propose and administer have to be very qualified. Korea's MTI has quality people as well, but owing to a shorter history and rotation, among other things, its impact falls short of its Japanese counterpart's. Administrative guidance really tests one's knowledge and relationship power, particularly because one cannot rely on legal enforcement. I recall that, in the old Ministry of Commerce and Industry in Korea, the occupant of the position overviewing the electronics industry changed twice. In contrast, some MITI bureaucrats have been involved with electronics for over two decades.

Korean achievement in the high-technology arena to date has been miraculous. And this momentum will continue into the arenas of biotechnology, aircraft and space technology, artificial intelligence, and so on. Much of this success has been due to the Korean ability to import technology, products, and know-how through means that are perhaps much more flexible than the Japanese would tolerate.

At the same time, structural change is necessary as Korea will be forced to move into higher-value-added product categories by other newly industrializing countries and by less-developed countries. The most significant issue in this realm is human-resource-related, and with labor problems, Korea needs to deal with this issue even faster than it would like. However, as mentioned before, the Koreans do have a remarkable ability to force an acceleration, so there is hope in this regard.

6

Japan: Korea's
Friend or Foe?

J apan and Korea have both been described as "followers"
of Western industry, and if that is an accurate portrayal,
it may be of use to understand how the two countries
cope with each other. Though it has not been a particularly
smooth relationship, there seems to be coexistence despite
uneasiness.

For better or worse, emotion plays a significant role in
international relations; it always has, it always will. From
this standpoint Korea and Japan have had a very delicate
relationship.

HISTORICAL FACTORS

It was noted that Korea had been a target of constant
intrusions by its neighbors. China and the Mongols tried
to conquer Korea a number of times starting from the
eighth century into the fourteenth. Japan has made its

share of attempts—the most prominent being Shogun To-
yotomi Hideyoshi's attack in 1592. There were several
attempts following this, including negotiations with China
on how to divide the Korean territories. Before Hideyoshi
could complete his invasion, he died. Tokugawa Ieyasu,
his successor, known to the West as "Toranaga" in James
Clavell's novel *Shogun,* was against the Korean invasion
for strategic reasons that had nothing to do with love
for the Koreans. Today some Koreans naively tend to
consider Hideyoshi to be the worst villain there is, and
Ieyasu to be a "good guy."

Even in the nineteenth century, Japan had always been
thinking of how to annex Korea. One of the prominent
politicians of the time, Itoh Hirobumi, who was the first
prime minister of Japan, was assassinated by a Korean
revolutionary, Ahn, in Manchuria because it was felt that
Itoh was one of the leaders planning the potential annex-
ation. They succeeded in 1910, and the occupation lasted
for thirty-six years. Any victim of an occupation tends to
feel that the aggressor was particularly cruel. It seems to
be the case, however, that Japan did leave rather bitter
memories of its cruelty toward the end of World War II
in quite a few countries. I have traveled extensively in
the Pacific Rim, and there is not one country where I
am not reminded of Japanese atrocities.

According to descriptions by Koreans who lived through
the Japanese occupation, the period was almost excessively
stringent. In the extreme, it would seem that the Japanese
wanted to eradicate Korean heritage and culture completely. They required the Koreans to use Japanese names.
They forbade the Koreans to speak Korean or sing Korean
songs. Those caught doing so were killed at times. I was
traveling through Kyushu Island in Japan and found a
map of Korea printed during the occupation. Interestingly,
many of the streets and locations in Seoul were renamed
to conform to the Japanese convention. Perhaps to the
Japanese this was a way to satisfy their strong need for
cultural homogeneity.

This era is, of course, still alive in the memories of those who lived through it. They are usually in top management. What contributes to their despisement is the occasional rationalization that Japan tries to provide. Once in the sixties and twice recently, a high-ranking official in the Japanese government made a statement to the effect that politics is a matter of power play, and that the weak party who allowed the intruder to take over is at least half to blame for what happened. One person to make that statement was Fujio, educational minister of Japan, and he was impeached. However, many Japanese critics added that the "Fujio statement" was probably a belief of the majority of the Japanese people of that generation. More recently, Okuno, the land minister, made a controversial statement along these lines, and he was forced to resign. Also, the Japanese tried to change their history textbooks so as to use a "weaker" word than *invasion* to describe what happened during that period ending in World War II. Many of my Japanese friends whose grandfathers and fathers were involved in these events have privately told me that in fact they were nothing short of invasions and massacres, but of course no one in Japan would admit that publicly.

Another factor that grates on the Koreans also relates to the interpretation of how the Japanese derived their civilization. What is in question is whether cultural influence came from China to Japan through Korea or not. Many Japanese claim that Korea had practically nothing to do with how Japanese culture came into existence. The wisdom in Japan is that all the cultural influences came by sea, in the form of either priests who made missionary visits to China or pirates who traversed the ocean. According to this theory, practically no cultural transfusion occurred by land.

In reality, however, when one goes down to Kyushu Island, which is physically the closest to Korea, and looks for various relationships, much may be uncovered in Japanese publications. First, Buddhism traveled to Japan partly through Korea starting around the fifth century. No one would doubt that Buddhism carried with it a whole set of values that still influences both societies rather strongly. Second, during the eighth and ninth centuries, when Korea was having internal revolutions that led to the unification of the country, Japan sent missionary forces to aid Paekche, one of the factions, in their fight against Shilla, another faction. During this era, much transfusion occurred—Dazaifu, one of the administrative centers of Japan during the era, had a Korean-style castle, Korean-style graves, and so on. And toward the end of the sixteenth century, Hideyoshi brought people skilled in pottery from Korea to Japan to transfer "technology" to the Japanese, who were behind at the time. A memorial to one of those imported pottery craftsmen can still be found in Arita, which is today one of the renowned centers of pottery in Japan. Perhaps the Kyushu people are a little less conscious of their pride when it comes to these historical ties.

This defensiveness on both sides is aggravated by emotion based on a lack of information. While books on the other country from a tourist point of view are widely available in both countries, there are still very few books that document these somewhat sensitive issues. And when one looks at Korean history books for descriptions of interactions with the Japanese, and at Japanese history books for descriptions of interactions with the Koreans, the explanations are so mutually exclusive it is mind-boggling. Perhaps the reader is starting to understand why the Japanese describe Korea as "the nearest and further country"—nearest physically, further in terms of relationship.

ECONOMIC INTERDEPENDENCIES

Despite all these biases, in business economic merit sometimes supersedes emotional obstacles. Both countries have called on the other to fulfill economic needs.

There are several types of economic relationship between Korea and Japan. First, there is Korea as a market for Japanese manufacturers. Second, there is the opposite, namely Japan as a market for Korean manufacturers. Third, Korea does much contract manufacturing for Japanese manufacturers. Closely related to the first and third relationships is technology licensing from Japanese firms to Korean firms.

Korea as a Market for Japanese Manufacturers

While Korea shows a trade surplus with the United States, its balance with Japan is significantly in the red. As mentioned previously, Korean manufacturers are heavily dependent on the Japanese for components and for equipment.

Korea may not have wanted to become this dependent on Japan. However, in the course of its development, for better or worse, it set up a very assembly-intensive structure with parts-fabrication expertise lagging far behind. Unfortunately, given this structure, the more one exports, the more one has to purchase from Japan.

Why Japan, then? First, in some cases, there are few or no alternatives. For example, it was mentioned before that Koreans are very active in consumer electronics. There are very few consumer electronics manufacturers left in the United States, and thus very few competitive components suppliers. Japan, being the most competitive country in this arena, would tend to have the most competitive suppliers to that industry. Also, if Japan is the target, why not try to integrate as much of its technology as possible? The limitations of this strategy were discussed earlier.

Despite many cultural and emotional differences, somehow the Koreans find the Japanese easier to deal with as suppliers than they do many Western firms. A good part of this is geographic proximity and being either in the same time zone or one hour apart, depending on standard or daylight saving time. Those who have dealt across the Pacific will understand this quite well.

Also, the Japanese do tend to treat their customers well. In the beginning, the Koreans were skeptical that the Japanese would provide good service to their competitors even if they were customers. But, as mentioned previously, large Japanese firms have autonomous divisions, and the components divisions may sell aggressively if there is economic merit even to the detriment of its sister consumer electronics division. Also, older Koreans speak Japanese, and ironically, due to the Japanese occupation, they understand Japanese psychology fairly well.

Recently, however, the Korean government has been quite alarmed by the country's import dependency on Japan. They have started a campaign to diversify the source of their imports to non-Japanese countries, particularly countries they may wind up having trade friction with. The government has asked each large Korean business to submit detailed plans on how much they will buy from countries such as the United States, and the European nations, and has led purchasing missions to those countries. Recently, one Korean executive mentioned that while the Japanese perform minimal amounts of customer training to make an equipment sale, the Germans are more generous in this regard, and thus he has made it a policy that even if the German pricing is 10 percent higher than the Japanese, he will still buy from the Germans.

As far as finished products are concerned, the Koreans seem to have taken the same strategy that the Japanese took in the past. They have basically split up products into several categories. For products such as automobiles and many consumer electronic appliances, where Korean manufacturers already have much know-how and already supply the domestic market, they made it very difficult for the Japanese to export to Korea finished products either through tariff or nontariff barriers. The second category is product areas that Korean manufacturers would like to enter and that the government feels are important for the economy, but where critical know-how is lacking. In such a case, the general scheme was that a Japanese firm must partner with a Korean firm—usually in a joint-venture fashion with technology transfer in order to participate in the marketing of finished products in Korea. In the last category there was no choice but to let foreign manufacturers bring in products, because there was such a need for the product domestically and not having the product would hinder advancement. Recently, however, Korea has been encountering much pressure to lower such limitations on the trade practices of its economic allies. As a result, the Korean government has liberalized many of these policies and has allowed many Japanese and foreign manufacturers unilaterally to sell their products in the Korean market. Yet, as one can surmise, these adjustments will require a delicate balancing of foreign and domestic interests.

Japan as a Market for Korea

Importation of Korean finished goods into Japan started quite a few years ago; however, there wasn't much interest until the appreciation of the yen relative to the won made Korean and other NIEs' goods look so inexpensive. The product categories that have aggressively made their way into Japan include jeeps, consumer electronic products such as VCRs, radiocassettes, electric fans, refrigerators, and videotapes; foods such as *kimchi* (Korean pickles) and instant noodles; cement; and semiconductors. However, there seems to be no limit to the list, as new products get imported almost every day.

As a person who has helped sell U.S. products in the Japanese market, I am continually amazed that the complaints Korean manufacturers make about selling to the

Japanese market are remarkably similar to those Americans have made. It is particularly fascinating because in the case of U.S. products, cost-competitiveness is often lacking, and thus the Japanese can claim that the product is not encountering any nontariff barriers. Korean products are quite cost-competitive—sometimes they are 30 to 40 percent cheaper at customer-pricing levels. Yet, apparently, the Japanese market seems to be rather difficult even to the Koreans.

Such difficulty seems to be inflicted by both the Koreans and the Japanese. The Koreans themselves need to adjust culturally to sell in Japan. According to those Koreans who are selling to the Japanese, particularly difficult are the Japanese consensus-decision-making methodology and the attention Japanese pay to details. Cosmetic irregularities and products that are not precisely to spec or as advertised may be thought of as nonissues in Korea, but are decisive buying factors for the Japanese.

On the Japanese side, there are those consumers who simply will not try Korean products no matter how inexpensive the products are or how good their quality is. It is something like what "Made in Japan" used to mean in the United States in the fifties and early sixties. Then, there are those people in the Japanese distribution channels who will not carry a Korean product no matter what. They are unsure of the quality of the Korean products, steady supply, and so on—all worries that also apply to an American supplier to the same Japanese retailer.

However, it seems that both Japanese consumers and distributors are slowly changing to a more pragmatic attitude. Japanese consumers, according to various surveys, are willing to buy NIEs' goods if priced 30 to 40 percent lower than their Japanese counterparts. They are becoming rather shrewd. They purchase Japanese goods when they need the high-end features; astute Japanese travelers are buying Japanese goods outside Japan. Japanese consumers also used to be stubborn about products that were perceived as even slightly unreliable; today they are starting to take on American influence—disregarding extended reliability since a certain part of their purchases are going to be replaced or discarded several years later anyway. While Korean imports into Japan are still small in quantity, they have been growing by multiples.

And some retailers are adventurous. JUSCO, a well-known retailer in Japan, has started a campaign called "Made in the World," which attempts to procure products from any country that offers quality value for money. They are rather pragmatic about it; they look for one of two conditions: The first is that a product from a newly industrializing economy such as Korea ought to be at least 25 percent less expensive than its Japanese counterpart. In other words, it has to be noticeably cheaper. An example would be a Korean compact refrigerator that sells for 70,000 yen as compared to 90,000 for a similar Japanese product. The second would be niche products, which have no direct Japanese competition. The popular example of this is the previously mentioned new-product category invented by a Korean manufacturer that could be called read-only VCR, a VCR that cannot record. The situation with this product is that while the least expensive Japanese recording VCR is priced at around 40,000 yen, the Korean-made read-only product is priced at 29,800 yen. JUSCO is quite shrewd in the appropriate selection of products for quality and price; the Korean products that they choose are sold out season after season. In the area of portable-radiocassettes, an electronics trade paper in Japan claims that the extent to which Korean products are affecting the Japanese market is still not completely visible due to contract manufacturing: it estimates that 70 percent of the radiocassettes sold in Akihabara—the electronics retail district of Tokyo—even under Japanese brand names, are made in the newly industrializing economies; perhaps fully half of them are Korean.

The Korean car is planned to arrive in Japan shortly.

As mentioned before, the Hyundai Excel became such a success in the United States because Hyundai was able to find dealers who would terminate their American or Japanese car product lines to become fully committed to selling and servicing Hyundai automobiles. American dealers are very independent, particularly careful not to yield purchasing power to their suppliers.

In Japan the situation is completely different. The Toyota Group, for example, has a dealer network subordinate to the affiliated sales subsidiary company, which depends in many different ways on the group itself. The linkage could be financial, such as the manufacturer carrying inventory risk, or other creative financing of working capital. It could be human-related; for example, there could be an ex-Toyota man in the dealership, or perhaps the president is a fellow alumnus of a Toyota executive. It could be operations-related—assurance of supply, priority of delivery, and so on. While these levers exist in the United States as well, the ties that bind the manufacturer and the dealer together are far stronger in Japan than they are in the United States. Such a dealership is not likely to switch over to a Korean manufacturer even if it is not completely satisfied with Toyota's policies.

There may be creative ways around this problem, however. It is reported that Mitsubishi Motors is seriously considering distributing Hyundai low-end automobiles in Japan. If a major Japanese auto manufacturer decides to carry an import, all the subsidiaries and affiliated dealer networks can carry that same import without being disloyal to the group.

Apparently the holding back of a more aggressive import drive into Japan of Hyundai cars has to do with the Korean side. First, success in Japan would be a direct result of dramatically low pricing resulting from cost savings. In 1989, Hyundai will be able to manufacture enough parts internally to avoid importing parts from Japan and therefore avoid paying the penalty resulting from the appreciation of the yen. Second, it is deemed prudent to watch the Korean labor situation, as labor unrest could cause interruptions in delivery to Japan. To the Japanese—who rely on supplier continuity—delivery interruptions by the Koreans would greatly discourage continued business relationships.

Even with adventurous Japanese like JUSCO and Mitsubishi Motors, it will take a while to penetrate this set of distribution channels, and success will take longer than in the United States. Yet one thing is clear: The Koreans can be culturally very Oriental when selling to the Japanese—they can bow quite deep; it doesn't hurt their egos as it would the Americans'. They will work unbelievable hours to cater to the Japanese purchaser; those types of hours would be impossible for an American firm or even its Japanese subsidiary. And they usually have a low-cost product with quality not far behind that of its Japanese competitors. If this combination doesn't eventually crack the Japanese market, then the verdict ought to be that the Japanese market is indeed closed.

Korean Firms as Partners of Japanese Firms

Despite all the emotional barriers, the economic merit of rushing to Korean subcontractors to counter the rapid appreciation of the yen is significant. During 1986–87, small-to-medium enterprises in Japan flocked to Korea even more aggressively than large enterprises because they had practically no other choice to stay afloat. Large Japanese companies, some of which I personally know had had bad experiences with Korean firms, still went back to Korea for renewed partnerships, albeit with different partners.

Also, various service sector firms such as banks and research institutes rushed to Korean and other newly industrializing economies to investigate their suitability for contract manufacturing. They looked at factors like real estate pricing and deal making, labor quality and wages, tax structure and incentives, existence of infrastructures, and availability of components and materials.

There are also other forms of partnership. It was mentioned that Mitsubishi Motors has a 10 percent stake in Hyundai Motors. After seeing that the Hyundai Excel was a success in the United States, it was reported that Mitsubishi requested that its Midwestern dealer network in the United States handle the Korean car. Then there is the vendor-supplier partnership. It was reported that the Goldstar Plant in Alabama, which produces color TVs, couldn't procure enough tubes from Korea—it was considering obtaining the parts from Toshiba Westinghouse, a competitor at the end-product level. Even more convoluted, Goldstar set up a joint venture with Thailand's Siam Cement to assemble color TVs. Siam Cement had set up a CRT (cathode ray tube) manufacturing company with the aid of Mitsubishi Electric, Toshiba, and Philips. Apparently the Goldstar–Siam Cement plant will use those tubes. Clearly, economic merit has a way of overcoming national biases.

Korea and Japan Competing in Third-Country Markets Such as the United States

The situation here is basically consistent with the indication given in chapter 3. That is, Korea's share in third-country markets is minuscule in general, but it has grown markedly in selected product categories such as VCRs and automobiles. It is said that Japanese manufacturers hold more than 90 percent of the market share in the U.S. VCR marketplace. Newly industrial economies as a whole held 1.1 percent in 1984; that figure grew to 3.6 percent in 1986—nothing to be scared about.

Yet there are product categories in which Japanese manufacturers are in fact becoming sensitive. According to JETRO (Japan's trade promotion organization), in the categories of stainless tableware, bicycles, toys, and color TVs, newly industrializing economies already hold a significantly larger share than do Japanese manufacturers combined in the U.S. market. Also, in the categories of TV tubes, steel, and other products, NIEs are about to overtake the Japanese share of the U.S. market. Admittedly, these are largely low-tech items. And it is the combined market share of the NIEs that's really worrying the Japanese, although it is true that the Koreans, being the most visible, are an easy target.

One amazing statistic that I heard recently is that in a high-tech product, namely personal computers, Japanese shipments to the U.S. market dropped 28 percent from 1986 to 1987, largely as a result of competition from newly industrializing economies. That seems plausible as most of the Japanese personal computers sold in the United States are IBM-PC compatibles. Not only do all four major electronics houses in Korea compete in these compatibles; major Taiwanese houses such as Acer/Multitech are pumping out these products in mass volume. In fact, some American computer manufacturers who used to subcontract IBM-PC compatibles from Japanese firms are shifting to NIE sources.

TRADE FRICTION BETWEEN JAPAN AND KOREA

As one might surmise, there is much debate on both sides about whether all of this is fair or not. We have noted that the two countries have significantly different cultures and share a not-too-harmonious history. In a situation like this it is only natural that there be some frustrations on both sides. Let us look at these in categories similar to the foregoing. What is indeed very interesting is that many of the arguments are déjà vu to a person familiar with Japan–U.S. trade friction.

Balance of Trade

The root of the problem is, of course, that the balance of trade is significantly in Japan's favor. In other words, the Koreans buy a lot from the Japanese, and the Japanese buy relatively little from Korea.

With respect to imports of Japanese products into Korea, the Japanese insist that their success in the Korean market is solely a product of the Korean industrial policy of promoting assembly operations. In other words, as stated before, the Koreans buy parts from Japan (among other places), assemble products based on them, and export to third countries. With this structure, the more Korea exports, the more Korea has to buy from Japan. And also, even as the yen strengthens considerably against the won, only a fraction of the exchange advantage can be realized. The Koreans really have not been able to argue against this except that the government there is embarking on a policy to diversify their components imports away from the Japanese.

The other half of the equation is imports of Korean products into Japan. Korea has claimed that Japanese import duties discriminate against Korean products—that, compared to an average import duty on all imports of 3 percent, Korean products are taxed at an average of 9 percent. In addition, it is maintained that Japan is not liberalizing those product categories in which Korean products are competitive.

As is the case with respect to arguments against U.S. trade negotiators, the Japanese have a whole battery of responses. The first is a detailed point, as is to be expected. According to the Japanese, the Koreans apparently made a mistake in calculation in coming up with the 9 percent— it is not a weighted average, just a simple average, thus not taking into consideration items that are not taxed or given preferential treatment. They add that 40 percent of Korean imports into Japan are not taxed, and that compared to Western nations, Japan has the least import restrictions on Korean products. Specifically, in the arena of textiles, it was claimed that apart from Switzerland, Japan is the only country allowing unrestricted textile imports. (It is interesting that in 1987, Japan asked Korea and other less-developed countries to exercise voluntary export restraints on textiles because they were hurting Japanese domestic textile producers.) Interestingly, this was at the same time that the Japanese were telling the U.S. semiconductor industry that U.S. customers were choosing the Japanese products because they were more competitive, and that the Japanese were not to be blamed for lost American jobs.

Another familiar argument is that Korean product quality and lack of marketing effort are the chief reasons for the low penetration of Korean goods into the Japanese marketplace. One could easily substitute the word *American* into the previous sentence, and it would also be an accurate quote of a Japanese government official. According to the Japanese, Korea should have the most advantage selling into Japan due to the Korean ability to speak Japanese, geographical proximity, labor-cost advantage, and the fact that many Korean products were designed with Japanese technology that conforms to Japanese standards. In any event, the Korean government has asked each Korean conglomerate to set up annual objectives regarding sales to the Japanese market, and in a couple of years, we shall perhaps understand how this will turn out.

Technology and Manufacturing Partnerships

Deals are frequently the target of complaints about fairness. The gist of the Korean argument is basically that the Japanese are closed with respect to their technology.

The Japanese have coined the phrase "boomerang effect" to signify that technology that they transfered to the Koreans or other newly industrializing economies will come back to haunt them in their home and third-country markets. The example that one perennially hears about is the Pohang Steel situation. In that case the Japanese did agree to transfer steel-manufacturing technology to the Koreans. The Koreans set up a modern steel facility that outclassed the then-existing Japanese plants, much as the Japanese steel plants built after the war had advantages over their American prewar counterparts. The output of the Pohang Steel facility has now made a considerable dent in the low-end steel market for Japanese producers. The Korean reaction to this is that the Japanese shouldn't and can't hold on to all segments of the market in the face of maturity—it is only natural in consideration of international harmony that they give up that segment.

A natural extension of this idea is the Korean claim that the Japanese only transfer old technology—and noncritical technology at that—to the Koreans. Now, to my mind, this is quite interesting since it is almost identical to arguments that have been made by some American scholars with respect to partnerships between Japanese and American firms. In a sense, in view of the "boomerang effect" and in valuing technology that was developed by sweat and hard work, it is probably prudent that the Japanese guard their technology as fervently as they do. And their strong community orientation, low turnover, and organizational cohesion allow them to control outflow of their technology much better than the Koreans or the Americans, who suffer unintentional outflow due to turnover (to mention only one factor). Yet, obviously, this tightness is starting to be perceived in the international context as being too self-centered and not being open.

Another facet of this argument is that when the Japanese do transfer technology, they do so to their advantage. A group of Korean executives involved in transfer of technology from the Japanese mentioned that they felt that the

Japanese found a great methodology for modernizing their own plants. The Japanese—who I know are supersensitive about depreciation costs of manufacturing equipment—tend to work with old equipment that is way past the point of zero salvage value because it reduces per-unit product costs. Of course, this slows down technology infusion, particularly of manufacturing process technology. In the experience of these Korean executives, the Japanese broke this vicious cycle by taking the old equipment, transferring that equipment into a joint venture—counting that as the contribution from the Japanese side—thereby winding up with a reasonable equity position based on equipment they were going to scrap anyway. And often, being good negotiators, the Japanese put relatively high value on this equipment being transferred. As is the case with most business situations, one never knows whether this was indeed a scheme or whether it just turned out that way, but it is clear how the situation was perceived. That is the beginning of international misunderstanding.

In the face of all of this rather aggressive posturing by the Koreans, the Japanese have not chosen to play dead. They have a whole battery of arguments, some of which make reasonable sense. First, they claim that Japanese technology costs the Koreans less than does equivalent technology from Western countries. In other words, the average royalties tend to be lower for similar types of technology transfers from Japan. In the days when Korean firms had to get technology deals approved by the Korean government, the potential Japanese partner would sometimes be told by the Korean firm that the royalty rates were considered to be too high by the government, with excessive foreign exchange outflow usually cited as the primary reason. The Japanese, experienced in such technology deals, will compare various analogous deals and usually come up with the above observation. Thus, according to Japanese logic, if the Koreans are paying relatively less for technology, the Japanese are being generous.

As to why the Japanese don't transfer state-of-the-art

technology, they cite lack of protection of intellectual property as a reason. It is a fact that until recently Korea was not part of the worldwide intellectual property conventions such as copyrights and trademarks. But I personally find it rather difficult to understand this argument for two reasons. First, Japanese industry has only recently started to campaign heavily with respect to intellectual property protection. And vivid in our memory are cases that allege that the Japanese copied American technology—the Intel-NEC microprocessor situation, the IBM-Fujitsu operating-system arbitration, and the list goes on. Protection of semiconductor maskworks (lithography patterns) was put in place as recently as 1985. Second, while it is quite honorable to say that Japanese industry is now in a leading position and should therefore provide exemplary conduct in terms of respect for intellectual property, in reality during this period, some large Japanese firms turned into net exporters of technology. In other words, they received more royalty income than they paid out in royalties. And they have been increasingly subject to intellectual property violations by less-developed countries. I strongly believe that this latter inglorious reason is why they are pushing so hard for protection.

It has also been stated that the willingness to transfer high-end technology to the Koreans is illustrated by the fact that the Japanese have the fewest export controls with respect to high-end technology. This statement was made in conjunction with the refuting of the implication that Japanese government has influence over technology deals pursued by Japanese private-sector firms. To put this matter in perspective, these implications were made prior to the Toshiba-COCOM problem (a Toshiba subsidiary passed high-technology submarine-related information to a customer in the communist bloc), and now the situation is completely different.

The Japanese would claim that the Korean perspective on technology deals is biased. Apparently, the managers involved in successful deals don't talk about them, and the managers involved in failures tend to get quite noisy. Apparently, too, there are statistics to indicate that the foreign country with the most researchers on exchange in Korea is Japan. All in all, the Japanese viewpoint is that the Koreans are taking too short-term a view of technology transfer.

Competition in Third Countries and Natural Segmentation of Industrial Activities

As mentioned before, the Japanese are in the short term more worried about the effect of competition from newly industrializing economies in third-country markets than in their domestic market. That obviously seems natural because they have more control over what happens in their own backyard than in the U.S. market. For example, a Korean firm in the United States could convince a dealer representing a U.S. or Japanese firm to work for it. Or a Korean firm could hire away an American executive versed in how to market Japanese cars in the U.S. marketplace. Neither of these would be very easy in Japan. This is basically because in the United States, both the distribution channel and employees of a firm are loosely coupled to the firm itself, whereas in Japan they are very tightly coupled.

The basic thrust of the Korean argument here is that the Japanese should give up the low-end segment of products and strive for a natural segmentation of low- and medium- to high-end product lines by moving upwards in the value-added spectrum. They are expressing regret at the appearance that the Japanese, while moving up the spectrum, are clinging to the low-end segment (something that I wish American firms were better at vis-à-vis the Japanese), making it as difficult as possible for the Koreans to wedge themselves in.

The Koreans cite a whole slew of tactics used by the Japanese to hold on. The first allegation is that the Japanese dumped to slow down Korean entry into third-country markets. Another is that the Japanese limited availability of critical components needed for Korean exports, thereby limiting their share abroad. Then there apparently are public-relations-oriented tactics such as spreading propaganda regarding the poorness of Korean product quality, or spreading rumors regarding weakness in the financial situation of a Korean company trying to export to the United States. There are also claims that the Japanese are engaged in lobbying activities that would make certain Korean exports into the United States unattractive.

The Japanese simply shrug off all these arguments by insisting that Japanese firms are so competitive that they are not in the least afraid of Korean firms. According to a survey recently conducted in Japan, Japanese executives are not even afraid of the "boomerang effect" from Korean manufacturers. They apparently are much more afraid of U.S. government and industry—amid some of the more visible controversies recently, U.S.–Japan confrontation has at least temporarily overshadowed anything to do with Korea with respect to the state of mind of Japanese executives.

The sum total of all the allegations on both sides is really a challenge that Japan should understand and live up to its responsibilities as an advanced nation. Japan was treated as an adolescent by the United States for a long time in terms of tolerating a "band of protectionism" approach for fostering competitive industry, helping with the defense of the general area from a financial standpoint, and so on. The Koreans are saying that it is only fair that Japan provide similar aid to its neighboring "adolescent" nations for the sake of stability in the Pacific region, given the fact that it has become the only unmistakably successful nation in the Asian-Pacific area from an economic standpoint. Out of this generality, the defense issue really sticks out like a sore thumb. Japan still spends around 1 percent of its GNP on defense and Korea—with a population one-third the size of Japan's, and a GNP approximately one order of magnitude less than Japan's—is shouldering the burden of protecting itself and perhaps buffering Japan from a rather aggressive communist nation that believes in very extreme principles. In addition, one could claim that the three-year commitment that youngsters in Korea are mandated to make to the military deprives not only Korean youth of a valuable three years but also Korean industry of the quality and quantity of human resources to make its organizations globally competitive.

Of course, the Japanese reaction to all this is that Korea is using Japan as a scapegoat for its own industrial problems, and that most of Korea's criticisms of Japan are based on emotion, not facts. After all, since Japan can't remilitarize, they have given some support in the form of technology transfer.

All this shows a very hypocritical situation in which both sides argue fervently that the other side is at fault but also understand, act on, and exploit the unavoidable business dependencies that exist. It's basically an "odd couple" that manages to live on.

My own view on whether the Japanese are afraid of the Koreans is that they are. But much of the fear is self-inflicted. One American friend knowledgeable in Asian business expressed it this way, "The Americans are motivated by greed; the Japanese by fear." While the observation is a bit extreme, it is generally true that Japanese organizations hardly stray from inertia unless really shaken by fear. The Japanese believe that the Korean threat will require rapid adjustment, and they are getting prepared for it subconsciously.

More specifically, however, several factors make it rather easy for the Japanese to be scared of Korea despite the fact that Korea is still peanuts compared to Japan. First,

Korea is to Japan as Japan is to the United States in a number of ways. The obvious one is that the Japanese were the attackers of the past, and the Koreans are the attackers of the present, with a successful track record in several industries such as shipbuilding, steel, and television. In fact, this is precisely the same manner in which the Japanese penetrated the United States—not across the board, but in several distinct, highly visible product categories.

Second, the Koreans are hungry and ruthless; they work much longer hours than the Japanese at much lower rates even after the labor strikes. Japanese managers are at the same time struggling with the generation gap they feel relative to their younger employees, who have a totally different work ethic—less work, more personal time. And Korean quality, which has been a differentiating factor for the Japanese for a while, has recently been improving. The Japanese are having a hard time facing maturity on the national life cycle, particularly because it basically occurred in the span of one generation. In other words, the people in top management in large Japanese firms saw the birth of an industry, its rapid growth, and now its transition to maturity. One must admit, that is hard to take in one generation.

But there is a factor that compounds all of this. Just the same way that the Japanese caught the Americans blind because most Americans couldn't read or understand Japanese while the Japanese studied American industry vigorously through the written media, most senior Korean managers understand and read Japanese thanks to the Japanese occupation, but the Japanese have just begun to read Korean. Perhaps they can use a little of their own advice to the Americans in terms of learning Japanese. Also, Korea is the only country in the much-paraded "group of four newly industrializing economies," including Taiwan, Singapore, and Hong Kong, that models its development on what the Japanese have done for the past three decades. The Koreans have studied the Japanese industrial structure, macroeconomy, along with the microeconomics of the individual firms with intense fanaticism. As mentioned before, this makes for an infrastructure in which any know-how that is obtained from the Japanese is almost instantly transferable and useful.

The Japanese, in addition, know two things only too well. First, a small production base on an absolute scale is not to be taken lightly, particularly when combined with a high growth rate—not to forget what they went through themselves. Second, they understand what the Tokyo Olympics did to benefit their economic development.

So they are scared. They are scared in the third-country markets, and they are really scared with respect to their own market. In third-country markets, they are aware that unless there is astute maneuvering, they will end up being "sandwiched"—high-end products either encounter stiff competition in the United States or end up being restricted through trade friction, and low-end products are attacked by the Koreans and other newly industrializing economies. While there are other areas in between these extremes, and other new arenas in which the Japanese are sure to be successful, it isn't clear how big those markets will be and whether they will be big enough to support the more than 100 million people living in Japan.

One can understand why they are scared with respect to their own market, despite the trivial market position that Korean manufacturers have today. When one looks at Japanese history over perhaps a two-thousand-year period, one notes that the Japanese have been "expansionist" on more than a few occasions. As mentioned before, they tried on numerous occasions to annex Korea and other countries, almost got much further than that in World War II, and after it became obvious that military expansion was not possible, they did so through trade. On the other hand, when one thinks carefully about Japan, the island nation, the ocean surrounding Japan has been astoundingly successful in serving as a barrier toward military, business, or cultural infiltration during that same period. In fact, I challenge the reader to think of one major foreign military or business infiltration (at the end product level) that happened to the Japanese in their two thousand or so years of recorded history. (The Mongols tried twice, unsuccessfully, in the thirteenth century, if that's any hint.)

This created an environment in which stability (previously stated as *anshinkan,* or peace of mind, in Japanese) and homogeneity became more valued than human life itself. One finds many occasions in Japanese history when people were executed because they disrupted the general peace and procedures and did not conform to the principles that make for a homogeneous society. Thus, not only have they not been infiltrated from a military standpoint, trade at large was forbidden for a two-and-a-half-century period since the beginning of the seventeenth century. And even during the past forty years of rapid growth, they have not experienced significant imports other than necessary raw materials. Thus, this may be the first time in history that they actually face the prospect of a more than minor business infiltration into their land. This is what probably is at the gut level of the attention and visibility that Korea is getting in Japan recently.

7

Korean and U.S.
Firms as Partners

THE EMOTIONAL FACTOR

By now, the reader is starting to put together many of the factors that drive Korean industry. We began with an understanding of the culture and then moved on to discussions of the government, economy, private sector, and relationships with Japan, in that order. Partnering with the Koreans is a subject that naturally follows such a sequence.

It is not an overstatement to say that people tend to trust others who share a similar culture, particularly a similar value system. An American executive who recently visited Korea said that he could "be himself" in Korea—something he could not easily do in Japan. In chapter 1 we discussed how perhaps through historical accident, the cultures of Korea and the United States ended up becoming closer than that of Japan and the United States. But there are several other reasons as well. First, language plays a key role in communication, which in turn plays a key role in any kind of relationship dynamics. As mentioned previously, it is much more accepted in Korea to study abroad in the United States than in Japan, and as a result, there are more Korean students in the United States. In addition, while both countries require their youngsters to learn English, the Koreans tend to be more outward and aggressive with respect to trying it, and tend to complete the learning curve faster. These two factors combine to explain why one finds so many more people in Korea speaking English than in Japan. Also, in Korea, they motivate people to take on American influence—Korean people from prestige U.S. schools are treated with respect and do get ahead. One hears all too often in Japan of situations where a returnee from the United States has adjustment problems, and becomes perceived as peculiar. The motivation works in totally different directions.

Another nontrivial influence that perhaps by now is a subliminal one is the fact that unlike Japan, Korea and the United States have never fought each other in the history of the two nations. If anything, during the Korean War, the United States came to Korea's rescue. It isn't that this historical fact by itself makes any difference— much more pervasive is the fact that there are both Japanese and Americans alive who still remember World War II. How does one trust a country that perhaps hurt—even killed—one's loved ones? The same problem hinders the relationship between Japan and Korea. When the current generation of top managers retires, the remnants of this historical tragedy will perhaps subside.

More relevant perhaps is business competition. Japan has been increasingly perceived to be a threat to American industrial well-being by some U.S. firms. It is easy to fall into the trap of feeling comfortable believing what I've heard a number of times in the United States: "The enemy (Korea) of our enemy (Japan) is our friend (Korea)." That's a bit naive, and I'm sure most readers wouldn't be swayed by such thinking. Another that ranks quite close in simplicity is that the combination of U.S. product technology and Korean manufacturing technology is the formula for beating Japan. I've heard this theory being advanced by Korean firms eager to enter into partnership with technology-rich U.S. firms. It may be important to note that in many of these cases, neither the U.S. nor the Korean firm has been seen ignoring a deal that made economic sense with a Japanese firm.

While it may be the case that the Koreans are relatively easier to deal with than the Japanese from an American perspective, this does not imply that the Koreans are easy to deal with on an absolute scale. I once had a chance to hear an American executive seasoned in negotiations with Korean firms speak on how to deal with the Koreans. The tone of his advice was that the Koreans had "extended ethics," were very influenceable, and that one had to be very, very careful in dealing with them. That doesn't sound much like business ethics American style.

It is clear that the Japanese and American business societies operate on very different ethical principles. One isn't better than the other; they're just different. Korea has yet another distinct standard of ethics. It is very easy to say that one's own ethical values are the best; that the other guy's are somehow unfair. It seems, however, that the best internationally experienced negotiators learn to live with such differences without making extreme value judgments.

There are several factors at work here. The first is clearly that the United States, Japan, and Korea are physically in very different situations. The United States is a relatively abundant country and used to have a standard of living far higher than that of Japan or Korea. When one is affluent, one can be generous, and one can act in a very gentlemanly manner. One doesn't have to stoop low and compromise one's composure. Yes, the Japanese are affluent today, but most of today's affluent were poor only a couple of decades ago. Their behavior hasn't yet adjusted to a point consistent with their wealth and maturity.

The Koreans are certainly not wealthy, and given the population density and instability as recently as the Korean War, it isn't inconceivable that they adopt a "do whatever it takes" type of attitude. I've observed the United States before and after the wave of oil shocks: clearly, this experience made the country painfully aware that it was constrained in resources. Somehow, prior to that period, the American people felt generous and looked at most situations as being positive. But, since then, my feeling as an outsider is that a different outlook seems to have come into place.

Another aspect is simply maturity. As countries become more advanced, their citizens become more sensitive to the sets of values adhered to by others. There are cases where sheer naïveté produces misunderstanding.

The third has to do with something called situationality. The Japanese value stability, and as a result they try to keep commitments in the face of some major changes in the environment. In this sense, the Japanese are dependable, at least on the surface. In my experience, U.S. firms tend to be fairly situational—a change of management impels a change in strategy, which in turn causes partnership arrangements to be modified. The Koreans tend to be fairly situational as well—at times even more so than American firms. As mentioned before, when the environment changes so frequently, and capitalizing on change is an important aspect of success, then situationality becomes fairly widely practiced. This is clearly an aspect that makes the Koreans somewhat difficult to deal with from an American standpoint and really tough to deal with from a Japanese standpoint. The issue, of course, is how one trusts someone who changes his or her mind all the time. I will comment a little later on what this implies in terms of the meaning of a contract.

In terms of ability to "influence," which is again a delicate subject, I would attempt to explain it in this fashion. This is certainly not a phenomenon that is only known in Korea. Korean bureaucrats are often given considerable latitude in the interpretation of the law. Depending on which way the interpretation goes, the results can be dramatically different. Just for the fun of it, a long time ago, I decided to try to get something done without "influence." I took into Kimpo Airport a Japanese consumer appliance for a relative of mine. I figured that in the worst case, I could just pay the tax, and that would be it, like going through Tokyo Customs. Here is what happened.

The customs inspector told me that the item was taxable and immediately had it taken to a different location. I followed him, without knowing what was going on, to a counter where I thought I was going to pay the duty. The clerk there told me that it wasn't possible to clear the item that day, and that I had to come back the next day. I told them I was only going to be in Korea for about four days on that trip. After significant pleading perhaps for about fifteen minutes, they took me to another office in another building.

They had finally decided to give me a break. They were going to calculate the tax—that took more than thirty minutes. When I was called, they told me that they were going to take 50 percent tax on the item there at Kimpo Airport and that I would have to go to another location distant from the airport and pay an additional tax. I asked what this tax was, and they said that it related to the fact that I had told them the item was for my grandfather. Apparently, if I were to use it, the tax would be unnecessary. So I responded that my grandfather and I would both use it—which was actually the case. They relented and let me go with a 50 percent tax, and I had to go to the bonded warehouse to pick up the item. The whole process took about an hour and a half. This same process for a taxable item entering Tokyo Customs takes about ten to fifteen minutes.

It doesn't take a genius to understand that this is a stupid way to go about this. Imagine if one were in the international shipping business and had to handle hundreds or perhaps thousands of items per day, what this would be like. This is what "influence" means. It could be in the form of position or political power or other methods. Needless to say, ethical and legal considerations (particularly the Foreign Corrupt Practices Act) can put the American firm in a real bind in these situations even when these methods can be classified as "facilitative."

To reiterate the point made earlier about maturity, Japanese society was like this—although perhaps to a different extent—some decades ago. Since then the combination of simple economic advancement and tightening up of bureaucracy so that there is less individual discretion has made for much streamlining.

Despite all this, it should be noted that in Korea there are individuals who conduct themselves and their business according to the standards set a number of centuries ago in what is called the *yangban* society. (*Yangban* is a sophisticated form of gentlemanship in which intellectualism and respect for others are key virtues.) Koreans are rather proud of that era, and when one deals with those individuals, it becomes very clear that being honorable is genuinely sought after.

Attitudes toward relationships: We have talked at length about the constant struggle and trade-off between emotional and rational factors in business. It is my view, however, that in most situations the latter override the former. One well-known American executive once put it this way regarding partnerships: "We don't have friends; we only have interests. And we can't tell our interests much beyond two years." That admittedly is a very "dry" way of looking at a relationship, perhaps one that Orientals would not feel comfortable with at the surface. Trust is always the foundation of Oriental relationships. However, further delving uncovers that in most circumstances the underlying motives that prompt major events in a business relationship—such as formation, expansion, and separation—*are* in fact based on rather "dry" factors such as level and timing of return, efficiency of the factory, acquisition of technology, posturing against competition, and so on. While some partnerships have been based on strong individual friendships, the great majority of those that are successful have a stream of economic benefits that accrue to both parties over time.

THE DRY BUSINESS TRADE-OFFS

Apart from some of the emotional reasons why Americans may feel comfortable dealing with the Koreans, from an economic standpoint it is usually much easier to close a deal with the Koreans than with the Japanese. When an American company compares a potential subcontracting or a technology licensing deal involving the Japanese with one involving the Koreans, it finds that the Koreans usually provide a better deal—that is, more value for less. This is obviously to be expected because the Korean "walkaway" value—the point in a negotiation at which the deal would not be worth it to the Koreans—is much lower than it is for the Japanese. First, the Koreans usually have much less technology to barter with, and much less pride. Second, they frequently have fewer alternatives than a Japanese firm. It could be that for a Japanese firm, partnering is only one of their strategic alternatives, while for a Korean firm without critical technology, there is no choice other than to partner with someone.

The power game: When one starts talking about dry economic merit, a basic principle is "shopping around." There are situations in which American firms have used a Korean offer to leverage a Japanese subcontractor. And, in fact, in some of those situations, the U.S. firm did indeed switch to the Korean firm. The opposite happens as well—when

Japanese firms play tough on Korean firms with respect to technology licensing, Korean firms leverage the Japanese by talking with American firms. And both U.S. and Japanese firms leverage the Koreans by pitting them against firms from other newly industrializing economies— whether Taiwan, Hong Kong, or Singapore. We touched on the issue of the relative merit of dealing with Korea versus other newly industrializing economies in chapter 3.

In a free market, this is only to be expected. But there are some limits to this flexibility that must be dealt with, and the limiting factor is continuity. It is a fact of life that wage levels will go up in any given country over time, and countries that are less advanced and mature tend to have lower wages. Thus, for a firm from an advanced nation that desires to subcontract aggressively, this could mean "country hopping." For example, a U.S. firm may use a Japanese subcontractor for a period of time, and when it becomes more advantageous it may perhaps switch to Korea and then to other Southeast Asian countries.

It seems that Japanese and U.S. firms have a different approach with respect to this issue. Not surprisingly, Japanese firms prefer stability and thus don't country-hop too much. For example, in the mid-seventies, when American semiconductor firms were looking for low-cost assembly capability in Southeast Asia, the Japanese preferred to keep their assembly operations within Japan. The Japanese argument was as follows: First, if the Japanese suffer a cost disadvantage in terms of wages, they can try to compensate for it by reducing labor content—in other words, automation. Second, there are logistical and coordination advantages to having one's assembly plant near the rest of one's operations. Third, one doesn't have to incur the additional overhead of dealing with a different culture, political instability, and labor practices. The Japanese only started two or three years ago to move their assembly operations to Southeast Asia because the cost differential, given the abrupt 40 percent rise in the yen, was so large compared with any of the other factors that they had no alternative in order to remain competitive.

Even in other industries, such as consumer electronics (in which they did move to Korea; for example, for subcontracting), the Japanese tend to keep the operations and load that factory with higher-value-added products, and open another plant for low-cost items in a country that has lower wage levels. Considering the advantages that sometimes accrue by having manufacturing plants close to the market, perhaps the Japanese approach makes a lot of sense.

Control and legal protection: An often-heard cliché with respect to partnering is "every time the Japanese emphasize trust and relationship, the Americans emphasize control." Certainly there is nothing more frightening to managers anywhere than operations that they gradually lose control over. Moreover, operating overseas is largely a function of managing uncertainty—a different culture, a different operating methodology, a different political and economic environment. And, in my experience, the only thing from which Americans can take comfort in such ambiguity is mechanisms that systematically assure control to the U.S. firm.

The problem in dealing in Korea is that by and large the control mechanisms that are most frequently relied on in the United States—ownership and legal protection— tend to work in very different ways from those expected in the United States. The typical tactic of majority ownership, in the case of equity participation or of a contract that covers every potential problem plus comfort, is that one can sue for breach but that this does not usually get the desired results.

I really should mention one caveat here. I'm not a lawyer, and a qualified lawyer really should be consulted in specific situations. However, some of these problems occur so often from a business standpoint that I wish to offer my perspective.

One exception to the failure of "American-style" control comes when the Korean partner has sizable business or other dependencies in the United States. If the agreement is enforced under U.S. law, and if such dependency could be used as leverage, then one is on home turf.

Yet, if this is not the case, I advance the following theory: In the United States, I once heard the proverb, "He who owns the gold makes the rules." In other words, power is derived from ownership and ensuing management control. In the Orient, however, I would rephrase this as: "He who runs the operations makes the rules."

Operational strengths: At least two categories of operational issues must be considered to manage effectively such an international alliance. The first is matching the mutual transfer of value. The second is matching exit costs.

Let me illustrate the first issue through an example. An American firm does a technology deal with a Korean firm. It could be a technology-for-royalty deal or technology-for-subcontracting deal, for example. Structurally speaking, usually in such a deal the transfer of technology happens over a very short period of time, perhaps several months. The Korean party has instant access to the economic value created by the transfer. Of course, a license could be terminated, but technological know-how has much secondary value. Both royalty payments and shipment of subcontracted units to the United States firm could occur way past the point at which technology transfer has ended. It is easy to see, then, that the power balance shifts dramatically after the first few months.

Thus, it is of the utmost importance to match the timing of the exchange—to spread the transfer of value to the other party over time so that the next piece of value gets transferred only after one receives significant value back. I have seen cases in which the American firm transferred everything—product technology, process technology, marketing rights, sublicensing privileges—all at once. If that type of structuring can be avoided at all, a big obstacle to a working relationship can be removed.

Sometimes, however, this turns out to be easier said than done, particularly given the nature of technological transfer. This is because a critical amount of technology has to be given on first transfer in order to be meaningful to the Korean partner. For example, there is always overhead information in product technology—in addition to the actual product-specific know-how, there may be design-methodology-related know-how. There usually is a lot more of this type of perhaps "hidden" know-how than one thinks. If one were to transfer a second product, usually these hidden know-hows are usually the same. A company doesn't change design methodologies for every single generation of product. Thus, the incremental value of the follow-on product is less than the value of the first transfer. And, of course, in order for the American firm to keep up the value of the product stream, it has to have a fairly high batting average in terms of commercializing "hit" technologies at frequent intervals so as to keep the Korean partner's interest. As difficult as it may be, one has to plan to keep the partner interested over time.

Secondly, exit costs are often forgotten. One never wants to think about divorce when getting married or while married. Assuming that sound business merit dominates emotional factors in a relationship, if one slips into a situation in which one is dependent on one's partner but in which that partner has very low switching costs, then there is very little to bind the relationship together. For example, let us assume that an American firm is dependent on a Korean partner to sell to the Korean marketplace, as sometimes mandated. Let us also assume that after a certain period of time, the technology that the American firm provided can be as easily obtained from another U.S. firm, perhaps a competitor. One can see how this could be painful. One way to get around this is to be realistic about it, and have both parties reckon with the fact that the relationship ought to be a temporary one before starting the relationship—that perhaps termination after three years is the best alternative for both parties, and may even out exit costs on both sides.

Third, another common problem that I observe which relates to strengths derived from operations is that when a joint venture is originally set up, the foreign partner may have majority ownership of the concern by perhaps a narrow margin. Let's say that two or three years go by, and the operating manager of the joint operation in Korea says that in order to maintain competitiveness and market share they need to expand their manufacturing facilities aggressively. And the Korean partner is willing to foot the bill.

The U.S. partner has a very different view of this. First, they have better use for their money than putting it into this joint venture. Second, they are more concerned about the return on their investment than sheer market share. So they don't want to put up the cash. Since, if the Korean partner makes the additional investment and the U.S. partner doesn't, the U.S. partner's ownership position has to go down, the U.S. firm tries to convince the Korean partner to make do with what exists and not make the additional investment. The operating manager, however, disagrees with this mode of operation violently. From the U.S. standpoint, one either loses ownership control of this venture or, if the persuading is successful, ends up with a discontented partner or a partner who might just be less competitive if the operating manager is right. A similar argument could be made about limiting the product scope within a joint venture of this sort. The trade-off between control and competitiveness is a tough one indeed.

Intellectual property: It is very easy to lose technological value when transferring technology. This happens in two fundamental ways. The first has to do with pricing of technology. It is complicated enough to determine the value of technology, so that one usually thinks to value only the basic technology. One American firm that has some experience in such transfers with a Korean firm says that one has to review carefully what the technology transfer entails. For example, resources must be deployed in the U.S. firm to organize the technology package with the appropriate documentation. There probably needs to be extensive training of the Korean partner's personnel in order for them to be able to get the technology up and running. There usually is a need for continuing technical support in order to maintain such capability. And updates to technology are usually needed to keep current. My general feeling is that U.S. firms end up charging too much for the core technology—particularly given the fact that in the case of a hit product, one has already recouped the entire investment many times over, perhaps based on domestic sales only. But they charge little or nothing for the technology peripheral to that core technology.

The second aspect has to do with the operational methodology of transferring technology. One can try to specify in the contract exactly what technology or know-how the partner gets and does not get. Yet, realistically, when it comes to executing the transfer of information, the technology transfer engineer from the U.S. (who is usually a couple of management levels down from those who negotiated the contract) doesn't have any notion of what the contract says and has often not seen it. Thus, when an engineer from the Korean partner says that they need more know-how because they can't get the technology up and running with what they've been given so far, the U.S. transfer engineer ends up giving the partner information not intended in the contract. What often motivates this is that the transfer engineer's performance is measured on how smoothly the transfer occurs.

Perhaps the biggest concern in the minds of American

firms is whether their intellectual property will be protected, in Korea anyway. This is an area in which Korea is changing rapidly. They have certainly had patent protection for a while, and now they have legislated respect for copyrights and trademarks. As is the case with all countries, one must register a piece of intellectual property with the local sources in order to get protection. It also used to be that certain conditions had to be satisfied in order to be able to license intellectual property such as a mandatory transfer of know-how from the American to the Korean firm. But that seems to have been loosened quite dramatically recently. As far as enforcement of protection is concerned, there are still problems, as any tourist to Seoul would recognize. My guess, though, is that there will be much more success in protecting such property in the industrial arena sooner than in the consumer arena.

Contractual control: Let us return to the issue of "control." From a business point of view, several problems must be addressed. The first is competition in one's own backyard.

Often, a subcontracting arrangement involving a technology transfer includes clauses that reflect the desires of the Korean firm to be able eventually to market the product worldwide independently. I know of such arrangements between Korean firms and both Japanese and American firms. Usually the subcontracting arrangement starts out being a captive deal—in other words, the total output of the production on that product is delivered to the licenser. The clauses that permit the additional flexibility frequently allow the Korean firm to market such products through their own overseas distribution according to a staggered introduction schedule. The idea is obviously that if there is enough lag time, the technology would be old enough so that one could control the level of technology at which Korean firms could compete in one's own backyard. Basically, this methodology is sound, except that again it behooves the American firm to keep its batting average high with respect to technological advancements.

Also, many U.S. firms have a tendency to misjudge the residual value of non-state-of-the-art, low-value-added technology. This misjudgment is often a reflection of the underestimation of the length of the tail end of the product cycle in such "nonexciting" product arenas. Finally, lest one forget, in limiting marketing rights one has to be extremely careful not to breach U.S. antitrust laws as they are extraterritorial—they apply to U.S. firms even outside the United States to the extent that any arrangements limit competition in the U.S. domestic market.

From the U.S. point of view, there used to be quite a few restrictions on how a foreign (non-Korean) enterprise could operate in Korea. The major ones were repatriation of dividends, corporate tax treatment, lack of access to incentives provided to domestic firms, and in the case of joint ventures, limitations on the percentage of ownership. Most of these have been eased significantly, particularly because the Korean government wanted to continue to induce foreign capital and technology into Korea in the face of competition from other nations. In 1980 the share limitation on joint ventures was released. Starting in 1984, the government only scrutinizes deals with foreign firms that are in industries on the "negative list." Many are industries not on this list and, barring bureaucratic incompetence, the deals are approved quite expeditiously. Around the same time, the foreign capital inducement law came into effect, and it had a number of results. It sought to reduce incentives that were preferentially provided to domestic firms. It provides for tax holidays on corporate tax for a number of years, yet some critics have argued that most foreign firms in Korea do not show much profit in their first several years of existence anyway. And the Korean government has removed financial restrictions such as remittances to the foreign parent company and dividend repatriation. Recently guidelines have been put in place that qualify foreign firms for the tax holiday treatment, such as the requirement that U.S. firms bring advanced technology to Korea or that if a plant is set up, more than 50 percent of the output be exported out of Korea.

In the end, there are several ingredients to a successful partnership with Korean firms. The first is that there be economic advantage to both parties over time, and that emotion play a subsidiary role to this. Much of the foregoing discussion could be construed by Koreans as excessive prompting of American firms to reduce their generosity with respect to transfer of technology. However, I truly believe that relationships that hinge on one-shot arrangements in which the American parties retrospectively feel that they wound up with the short end of the stick are actually bad for the Koreans in the long run. Thus the economic exchange has to be properly valued on both sides and mutual interest maintained over the life of the relationship.

Second, if the U.S. partner maintains personnel locally in Korea to help in the partnership, it is usually optimal if they can work with Koreans who are astute in local relationships. There are a number of reasons for this. Expatriate employees in Korea tend to be left out of certain social interactions during which misunderstandings are sometimes hashed out. Also, if there is any type of problem that risks exposing the partnership to legal difficulties, an independent opinion is needed first, and then, needless to say, the outcome can sway dramatically depending on the access someone of that sort has to the local authorities. Today, such a person ought to be a "graybeard" who listens a lot before making very focused statements, and who has a military or political background, meaning linkages into the bureaucratic power base. This—combined with frequent U.S. management visits that could be used strategically as an occasion for breaking impasses and building personal linkages—is recommended.

Last, both sides usually put insufficient resources and

effort into managing a partnership of this kind. I once heard a consultant say that it takes as much management time, energy, and resources to manage a partnership as it takes to manage a total division in one's company. That is somewhat counterintuitive, since the whole idea of a partnership is efficiency and synergy caused by the merging of two sets of capabilities. Although this efficiency may be true from a functional capability standpoint, whatever gains one gets from the fact that not all the work has to be done by one partner are usually offset by the communications overhead required to keep both partners' perspectives and strategies aligned and to arbitrate differences in opinion. Very often, though, I see situations in which the Korean partner will naturally have a whole division overseeing the partnership, if only because that is the only way they can compete in that product line. On the other hand, to the U.S. firm, that partnership could be a very small part of their overall game plan, and as such could be perceived as something that requires a couple of people's worth of investment. Such uneven loading of resources unfortunately creates a situation in which, first, execution of projects according to the contract becomes difficult even given the best intentions of both partners; and second, the American firm could wind up losing a lot of value in the process. American firms have been criticized a lot recently concerning their ability to implement manufacturing programs, for example. While this problem is being addressed, one ought not to forget that there is an important execution element to partnerships that also deserves serious attention.

In any business endeavor there are many good ideas, but only a few of them ever create real economic return because most fail in the implementation stage. It is clear in my mind that Korea offers much opportunity to the American firm—its manufacturing competitiveness, infrastructure, an educated labor pool, and so on. There is clearly value there. But one can as easily lose the value that was conceived depending on how one goes about setting up the partnership and how one implements the joint programs. I am convinced that in the end, only through careful consideration of these two elements can there be long-lasting, mutually beneficial relationships that can be construed as positive-sum arrangements. And that is the only way in which Korea can remain economically viable in the long term.

The Future of Korea
and the Korea–Japan–U.S.
Trilateral Relationship

Having discussed the development of Korean business and its bilateral relationship with Japanese and U.S. businesses, natural curiosity drives one to speculate on what is in store for Korea in the future. The Korean government has done some projections we shall look at. At the same time, Korean government and business will have to overcome a number of hurdles. And, finally, since it should be clear by now that the welfare of the Korean economy depends significantly on its trading partners—particularly Japan and the United States—let us extend our previous discussions on the bilateral relationships between these countries to a look at the trilateral relationship.

WHAT DOES KOREA LOOK
LIKE IN THE FUTURE?

Various governments, including those of the United States and Japan, have published reports portraying what their economies will look like in the year 2000. Korea has followed this cue, and in 1986 the Korea Development Institute, a government-related economic think tank, published a report called *Korea Year 2000*. This certainly presents one view of the Korean future.

Profile of Korea in the Year 2000

First and foremost, KDI has done some extrapolation on GNP in the year 2000. They assumed that the Korean GNP would grow at a compounded annual rate of 5.6 percent until 1990 (which could be a bit on the low side given actual growth rates for 1986 and 1987), and 8.2 percent for the following decade. This brings the size of the Korean economy in 1984 constant prices from about $81 billion in 1984 to $248 billion in the year 2000. A proper perspective on size is very crucial to setting the appropriate trade policies. Recently, there has been a lot of talk about whether the world should become tough with respect to the Koreans. One faction says, "Korea is peanuts, leave them alone." The obvious counterargument uses the example of Japan: "They used to be peanuts, and look how fast they grew." The amount of $248 billion is approximately four times the size of IBM Corporation, a single U.S. company today. In 1985 the U.S. GNP was $3.8 trillion; the Korean economy will be $248 billion in 2000. Let's compare this to Japan. According to *Economist* magazine of Japan, Japan's GNP will be approximately $3.5 trillion in 2000 assuming 3.75 percent growth until 1993, and 4.25 percent growth thereafter till 2000. Thus, the Korean economy will not even be 10 percent of the Japanese. Anyone who understands the advantage of early entry into an industry understands this phenomenon. The earlier one gets started, the earlier one's revenue base becomes bigger, and thus, even if the growth rate of a latecomer is significantly higher, catching up on absolute terms is rather difficult.

Korea's population is fairly well under control. In 1986 the figure was 38 million. In the year 2000, it is expected to be 49 million. Two aspects of this are important. As mentioned earlier, controlled population growth is central to the stability of economic growth. However, one Japanese executive got me thinking about something interesting. Japan, which has also based its economic development on human factors due to a lack of resources, has about three times the population of Korea. Consequently the supply of labor resources is also much higher. Thus, Korea will either have to boost the proportion of its population entering the labor pool or find an alternative path that reduces output dependency on the population, such as automation.

An aspect of this that deserves a little further study is what is called the population pyramid. This pyramid is basically a graph that plots the percentage of the male population by age group on the left-hand side, and the female population on the right. It is well known that Japan is concerned about its aging population. When a country is "young," the pyramid usually looks like an actual pyramid or triangle, with most of the population concentrated in the younger age groups. When a country starts to mature, the graph starts to take on more of the shape of a rocket. Later in the country's life cycle, the graph starts to look like a rectangle. Looking at the pyramids of the Japanese population in 1920, 1985, and 2025 presented in a booklet by the Keizai Koho Center of Japan, one sees precisely these three shapes. An analogous graph appears in *Korea Year 2000*, showing the pyramids for Korea in the years 1980 and 2000. Amazingly, the pyramid for Korea in the year 1980 looks like that of Japan in 1920, except that the base of the Japanese pyramid is wider than Korea's. Obviously, the Korean War had something to do with this. Even as forecasted for the year 2000, Korea's pyramid just barely starts to show some narrowing of its base. Thus, it's going to be a long time before Korea starts to see problems like those Japan is experiencing in this area.

We noted earlier that the Korean economy, like that of Japan, is exceptionally competitive in a limited number of product categories. Looking at the composition of Korean output over time and into the future indeed shows the effects of Korean industrial policy and the move into higher-value-added, knowledge-intensive industries. In 1981, for example, textiles were by far the largest industry in Korea. By 1990 the electronics and machinery industries will have come close to the scale of the textile industry. By the turn of the century, the electronics industry is projected to be the unquestionable leader in terms of size. It is interesting that in Korea, the automobile industry continually trails the electronics industry, whereas in Japan, the electronics industry recently surpassed the automobile industry.

In the case of Japan, its trade surplus relative to the United States is massive, and at the same time—in the certain industries it has focused on—has had a profound effect on the welfare of that industry. While Korea's overall output is not going to be as significant even in the year 2000 on a relative scale, there is still the worry that Korea may take away jobs in the specific industries on which it embarks. Anxiety along those lines would be pronounced if the overall world demand in that category does not grow. If electronics is an example of targeted industry, one can obviously expect fairly healthy demand increases over the long term.

The KDI report is quite all-encompassing in its vision for the year 2000; we have looked at some key aspects of the findings. However, simple extrapolation does not say much about some potential obstacles that stand in the way of achieving the profile described. Let's shift our focus to some of these challenges.

Some Future Challenges for Korea

So far, the consensus among economists seems to be that Korea has done a good job of developing. Many less-developed countries are studying Korea to see how much of it is applicable to their own case.

By way of review, a number of factors have contributed to this immense growth. The first would be low-cost labor combined with the "Confucian" emphasis on education. A country without natural resources had to utilize its human resources to its maximum capacity—this combination allowed it to do so. Second, industry concentration that is close to an oligopolistic structure—that is, a few large conglomerates competing fiercely in domestic and export markets—allowed Korea to optimize scale efficiency and kept the conglomerates honest by requiring them to compete. Third, Korea's aggressive pursuit of export markets required that its manufacturers become world class rapidly, otherwise they wouldn't be competitive enough. And, finally, its cultural flexibility, particularly when it comes to procuring from other countries what it direly needs to develop, played an important role. Examples would be negotiation skills when it comes to acquisition of foreign technology, and the rights to host the Olympics.

So far, these factors have served Korea well. Yet the global environment is changing. And along with it, Korea needs to align its strengths and capabilities in order to cope. Let's look at what some of these are.

Political and financial issues: In particular, stability is key since even when a military-related government has been in power for over two decades, there have been marked discontinuities including several coups d'état. While it is clear that democracy means different things in different countries, in the broad sense, Korea cannot avoid facing up to this challenge. Many specific issues relate to this, such as civil rights, legal protection, and education, but in the context of business, how one evolves trade policy as continual democratization unfolds is a key challenge. As mentioned before, it is clear to a great many people that the economic policies of the past two decades have by and large been very successful and have contributed on the whole to the Korean economy. This is in spite of the fact that, for example, many small to medium-size businesses have suffered due to discriminatory practices favoring large business. Yet, overall, one could persuasively argue that the scale advantages of large business have certainly benefited the Korean economy as a whole. Just imagine if in the name of democratization, large business rapidly became a target of dissolution: The country could be in serious trouble. Thus, change in moderate steps toward democracy, implying a stable transition, would be a key success factor for Korea.

A related factor that is not so easy to reconcile is the North-South relationship and the importance of the military in Korea. It certainly seems that the two Koreas have tragically become so distant in terms of their values and ideologies that logic proves fairly ineffective when it comes to trying to compromise to a mutually satisfactory solution. My belief is that the only way the two Koreas will move closer to each other is when the military balance between the North and the South is near even or worse for the North, and when the North Koreans come close to becoming economically unviable. An added bonus would come into being if neither the People's Republic of China nor the Soviet Union would even consider backing a North Korean military attempt on the South. In this set of conditions, which is realistically conceivable, even irrational leadership in the North would realize the futility of attack and the potential benefits of cooperation. The bottom line is that while political factors play a key role in the strained relationships, the two factors that will prove most important are the military balance and the economic needs of the North. Unfortunately for Korea, until economic dependency stabilizes the relationship between the two Koreas, military defense and deterrence capability would have to be maintained, just as SDI played a significant role in bringing the Soviets back to the bargaining table in order to resolve the INF treaty.

A strategic step South Korea is taking in conjunction with the Olympics that will aid in neutralizing the North is promoting trade and economic ties with the People's Republic of China, the Soviet Union, and other Eastern Bloc countries. South Korea's trade with the PRC is said to have been $2 billion in 1987 and is growing at a rapid rate. Although formal diplomatic ties do not exist yet, trade offices are being established and economic cooperation effected; examples are Daewoo's $10 million refrigerator plant in the PRC and Jindo Fur's plant in the Soviet Union, whose output is expected to be $20 million per year. It is clear that South Korea will have to tread carefully in this arena in order to avoid provoking the wrath of its current economic allies and to prevent COCOM violations. Although South Korea is pursuing economic deterrence with North Korea and other countries, for now the need to maintain military deterrence seems to be an unavoidable reality.

This is easy to say, of course; however, the implications on the political scene and the financial impact of military spending are severe. First, there is constant movement to reduce military power with the persuasive rationale that while the military brings with it defense capability, it also encourages and harbors power that is sometimes construed to be unfair. While perhaps that is good from a checks-and-balances standpoint, if one does stray to the extreme, then the delicate military balance between the North and the South could change. I must admit that on this issue, having spent a good amount of time outside Korea, I am probably less sensitive to the trials of putting up with the "hassle" of military power day in and day out. Second, it was mentioned that the South was running a tight ship with respect to financing its industry (in addition to the government and military) through external debt. This is clearly a tough juggling act.

Needless to say, additional financial issues will surface as challenges. To a large extent, the financial markets in Korea have been managed. Foreign exchange is not liberalized; the exchange rate is set artificially; the stock market is not liberalized; banking is regulated. Such management is perhaps what made this tight finessing possible.

But all of this managing is subject to foreign pressure, as trade issues are. Korea is constantly pressured to appreciate the value of the won, which would make their export products relatively less competitive. Restriction on foreign exchange is being criticized by businesses that want to trade internationally, particularly foreign entities that seek to do business in Korea but have no way to repatriate their funds and recoup their investment. Investors want to partake of the equity growth that Korean firms have been enjoying. Foreign banks are having a tough time competing in Korea based on the limited scope of business allowed. Clearly, all of this cannot last forever. Thus, Korea will have to live with less control over and more uncertainty about its own financial situation in the years to come. While the Japanese had more "cushion" in the financial realm due to higher savings and lower defense spending, the Japanese experience relative to liberalization of the financial markets certainly is not very positively exemplary.

Yet opening up of the financial markets is going to be a significant challenge for Korea. Unless capital availability and supply improve dramatically, liberalization will result in intolerably high market interest rates. Korea would have to earn foreign exchange, save significantly more, and recycle those funds into the financial markets in order to alleviate the crunch that exists today. As financial institutions are state-controlled, many loan officers have been conditioned to lend money based on government direction rather than through economic merit. Nonpreferential borrowers of money tapped into the underground financial market. Trying to untangle this situation so that adequate funds are recycled in a formal manner will probably require a delicate balance between pressure and finesse. Otherwise, pandemonium could strike.

Let us move on to the problems that Korea will encounter in which the Japanese experience is instructive. One could easily say that Korea gained significantly from studying the Japanese economic methodology. Perhaps it isn't quite so simple as mimicry, but there is much value to be had just in knowing that a certain development strategy didn't work. As in any situation involving a leader and a follower, the follower reaps benefits from not having to go down blind alleys due to "limited" hindsight. It is interesting to view Korea's challenges from this perspective. Let's start with domestic issues. If human resources are touted as a significant Korean asset, we must look at what the future holds here.

Human-resource-related issues: As mentioned before, Korea has approximately one-third the population that Japan has. While a one-to-one comparison cannot be made, the supply of human resources is also smaller as a result. Unless Korea embarks on a policy that reduces human content drastically, finding a sizable number of well-educated people would be a key success factor.

Until the present, the literacy rate has probably been the most important benchmark of labor viability. As long as one is involved with very simple assembly operations that require reading and understanding instructions and perhaps a little arithmetic capability, a fairly basic educational level is adequate. Yet, as technology levels even in the factory become more advanced, and as Korean industry is pushed by other low-wage nations to move up the value-added scale, workers themselves have to be much more educated. I have toured numerous Japanese and Korean factories and have found that workers in a well-run Japanese factory, even in a location out in the countryside, always impress me not only with their grasp of the operation of their own stations but with fairly in-depth understanding of the overall manufacturing flow. Clearly, this is much more than simple literacy.

When one moves into the white-collar arena, the problem is even more acute. We discussed how until this stage of industrial development, some bright people at the top combined with average but obedient subordinates have constituted a viable setup. This is all right as long as one imports know-how from foreign countries and manufactures according to it without much modification. In other words, implementation of static knowledge can occur in this manner. Yet, as soon as know-how has to be evolved and turned into so-called dynamic knowledge—a process the Japanese carry out so impeccably well—much more outstanding people must enter the white-collar workforce. The first step in this has to be to raise the proportion of people who advance to university education. In that sense the Koreans are on the right track. Yet many Japanese and American businesspeople whom I know have expressed their concerns about the sometimes inadequate level of their Korean counterparts, and many of these feelings come from this phenomenon. This is probably one of the most important hinge factors that will determine whether Korea will indeed become an advanced nation or not.

Having talked about blue- and white-collar human resources, it is natural to touch on labor-management relations. The year 1987 marked an explosion in tension in such relations. As in any country, one basic cause of this has to be distribution of wealth. While there is always a gap between the compensation levels of the blue- and white-collar employees, when this gap becomes excessive,

strife breaks out. It is unnatural for workers to see the
company they are working for prosper, the environment
in which they live improve, and yet individually live under
intense pressure relating to personal finances and work
practices. This is perhaps a point of distinction between
the Japanese and the Koreans. Japanese white-collar employees even today live under very modest conditions;
moreover, the very product that they manufacture in their
own company is most expensive in their own marketplace.
The key difference here is that while Korean management
is largely still family owned and thus considered to be
"rich," the difference in compensation between the new
college graduate and high-level management is probably
lowest in Japan among the advanced nations in the world.
In addition, in Japan, employees whether they are university graduates or graduates with advanced degrees, are
compensated at roughly similar levels. In Korea, the difference in pay between a high school graduate and a university
graduate can be wide. Added to this, Japanese culture
reinforces stability in the sense that all share the fate of
the "group" (organization), and they have to sacrifice in
order to ensure a viable future. Perhaps when professional
management (as opposed to owner-managers) becomes
prevalent in Korea, some of these pressures will subside,
as long as management can peacefully coexist with the
workers.

All of this, however, says that while labor-management
strife could be stabilized, management will have to make
some concessions with respect to work conditions, practices, and wages. This will not come free and, combined
with the appreciation of the Korean won, will have a significant impact on the relative competitiveness of Korean
goods. Not to mention competing newly industrializing
economies such as Taiwan, there are other countries in
line such as Malaysia, Thailand, and of course the People's
Republic of China. Korean industry will be forced to move
up the value-added chain, and the more it does so, the

more it will risk colliding with higher-end marketplaces that advanced nations value highly.

Development of local demand: As customers start to demand high-technology products with more customization, it is increasingly important to be close to the customer. In the case of the Japanese semiconductor industry, for example, most of the users of semiconductors are there within Japan. Some of these users are probably the most advanced users of semiconductors in the world. It is from this application base that new semiconductor products can be innovated.

The Japanese made a very effective transition from the condition in which their thrust was export-driven to the point at which income elasticity of demand went up and as a result a domestic market for products emerged. While the demand levels are still not considered to be satisfactory, they are at least at the level where innovation can occur.

Korea must develop this type of demand in order to continue to prosper with respect to technological progress. The Japanese have become quite adept at producing what are known as application-specific integrated circuits—components that are specifically designed to control VCRs, for example. The amount of know-how in this arena is quite mind-boggling. This whole category of expertise is unfortunately missing in Korea because of the tight interaction that is required between the supplier and customer. This type of expertise is what drives the competitiveness of the finished product as well, so it is quite mandatory that the know-how be acquired, or else Korea risks falling behind.

Developing a supplier-contractor base: Let's take as an example Kyushu Island, the southernmost large island of Japan, known as Silicon Island. Anyone who has been there knows that fabrication facilities for semiconductors are only the tip of the iceberg. For every one of these plants, there are many suppliers and contractors. Every material supplier has set up shop near every major facility, and there are assembly contractors all over. As I recall, most semiconductor plants utilized on the order of ten subcontractors for assembly purposes—some of them wholly owned, some of them arm's-length entities.

In Korea there are still some major restrictions in terms of the necessary infrastructure. In the arena of printed circuit board assembly, which is a key capability for personal computers and other products, electrical components are mounted on a bare printed circuit board. These boards have become extremely dense—eight to ten layers are becoming fairly common. But until just recently there were no bare-board manufacturers in Korea that could provide eight-layer bare boards. Thus assemblers had to buy such boards from foreign suppliers.

There are some disadvantages to buying externally, as the Japanese have been saying for a long time (and the Japanese have been criticized for being too self-sufficient and therefore a closed market). Yet logistics and service capabilities are often limited when working over long distances. The business culture could be different, leading to unnecessary misunderstandings. And last, there is much lost opportunity in terms of joint development of products that cater to the needs of the Korean user along the lines that were mentioned previously.

Having subcontractors in the general vicinity of one's operation is also very convenient. Subcontractors can cushion the effects of discontinuities in demand conditions and can also lead to cost efficiencies in terms of minimization of complexity through off-loading of low-volume products. These are all capabilities that Korea must develop in order to become as robust a high-technology economy as Japan is. In fact, one of the reasons the Japanese have been able to weather the rapid appreciation of the yen has to do with the ability of all these entities in the manufacturing chain to share the pain instead of one assembler, for example, having to stomach it all.

The move up the value-added chain and specialization: During the era when labor costs were indeed a key advantage, Korean conglomerates could diversify into any arena that could leverage this labor advantage, and produce competitive output. As other less-developed countries are able to bring to the party even lower labor costs, Korea must move up the value-added chain into higher-technology products. These new arenas require that massive investment be made both from the R&D and capital expenditure standpoints.

As one looks at Korean conglomerates, on the whole they are much more diversified than their Japanese counterparts. I do not know of many Japanese conglomerates that simultaneously run a newspaper company, a hotel, a department store, golf courses, aircraft businesses, consumer electronics, and so on. Given the fact that Korean conglomerates are much, much smaller than their Japanese counterparts, it would make sense that in order to be competitive, the Korean conglomerates need to focus their relatively smaller available funds into a few strategic businesses. One simply cannot expect to be competitive on a global basis in thirty different business categories.

These improvements will not be easy for Korea to make. All of these adjustments have taken the Japanese a minimum of more than a decade. And, as the Japanese example has shown, overcoming these adjustments does not guarantee harmonious coexistence in the international context.

KOREA, THE UNITED STATES, AND JAPAN—THE TRILATERAL RELATIONSHIP

In the previous chapters, we have looked at the bilateral relationships between Korea and Japan and between Korea and the United States. The following table illustrates these relationships and in addition looks at the relationship between the United States and Japan:

For —— ——— is	Korea	Japan	United States
Korea	—	(Market)* Supplier of technology	Market Supplier of technology Source of capital (lender)
Japan	Market Subcontractor	—	Market Supplier of technology Borrower of capital
United States	Subcontractor (Market)* Borrower of capital	Supplier of technology Supplier of components, products, equipment (Market)* Lender of capital	—

*( ) indicates factors that are worth noting but relatively small.

Let me offer two points of clarification on the matrix. First, only major relationship factors are shown. Any bilateral relationship between countries spans many different types of activities. Second, factors in parentheses are those that are worth noting but relatively small. For example, Japan is a market for U.S. goods, but it is widely recognized that the size of that market is not yet as big as the United States would like.

A number of points emerge from the matrix:

1. The United States is a significant market for both Japanese and Korean products.
2. Japan has sold aggressively into both the U.S. and Korean markets, yet U.S. and Korean participation in the Japanese domestic market is still small.
3. The United States and Japan are heavily dependent on each other. The United States is a necessary market for Japan, and Japan is a necessary supplier of end products to U.S. consumers and of components and equipment to U.S. industrial manufacturers.
4. Korea has become a key factor in the structural adjustments taking place resulting from the maturing of the U.S. and Japanese economies. It adds significant value to U.S. and Japanese firms in terms of low-cost, reasonable quality subcontracting.
5. Korea is a small market for U.S. goods, primarily because of various restrictions.
6. In many product categories, Korea is able to acquire technology from either the United States or Japan.
7. A significant portion of Korea's external debt is held by U.S. financial institutions.

Diplomats from all three countries like to say that the relationship among the three countries is and will be harmonious. That is certainly a bit of an overstatement, and at the least, all three countries will have to make some adjustments if that noble goal is to be reached. Let us turn our attention to what these adjustments might be.

Dealing with the Market Problem

The first problem is closed markets. Whether the Japanese and Korean markets are closed or not, they are perceived to be. Korea will probably have to open its market at a faster rate than the Japanese due to the preemption factor mentioned before. In fact, Korea should open its markets as the Germans did—first removing tangible barriers to trade, including restrictions on participation, tariffs, quotas, and bureaucratic processes required for clearing and inspections, and then nontariff barriers. To export aggressively into other markets while limiting access to one's own market tends to be interpreted as unfair. And, after all, it is difficult to criticize the Japanese for their seeming defensiveness with respect to their market if one's own is even more closed. Having said this, I would advise American politicians and businesspeople not to overestimate the Korean market. Korean per capita income is still quite low.

Assuming that this liberalization of the Korean market occurs at an acceptable rate, let us shift our focus to the Japanese marketplace. It is interesting to note that while the Japanese have exported aggressively to both the U.S. and Korean markets—countries with whom they run a significant surplus—it is no secret that relatively there are very few American or Korean products in use in Japan. Having personally experienced trying to sell American products in Japan, I know that often the Japanese tend to not be satisfied with the price, quality, delivery, or service of American goods. Today, in the product categories in which Korea is competitive, the price of a Korean product is usually at least 30 percent lower than the corresponding Japanese product, quality is often within the acceptable range, meeting delivery deadlines is not too difficult because of the much smaller distance involved between Korea and Japan, and service tends to be more in the Japanese than the American style, because—ironically—it was learned from their old colonial masters. Thus, the Korean effort to sell in the Japanese marketplace should in theory be met with much less criticism than its American counterpart. The United States, in turn, should use this phenomenon to its advantage by observing the degree of success of the penetration of Korean products into Japan. That would be another very valuable data point in assessing the real possibility of the opening of the Japanese marketplace. If the Japanese will not accept Korean products, then the verdict will have to move much more toward the belief that Japanese *anshinkan* is overdemanding to the point of cultural exclusivity.

Creative Use of Korea's Already Critical Role in Global Adjustments

On another note, some partnership arrangements could be made that take even more advantage of the fact that Korea is already a key factor in the structural adjustments taking place. The headline of the *Japan Economic Journal* dated March 10, 1988, mentioned a joint venture arrangement between Toshiba of Japan and Samsung of Korea in the area of VCRs. In a nutshell, the article reported that two joint ventures would be formed between the two companies. This arrangement has the potential of benefiting the United States, Japan, and Korea.

Before explaining the joint venture setup, let us look at Toshiba's situation. First, Toshiba has a VCR factory in the United States in order to manufacture products for the U.S. market. However, that factory had apparently been running at much less than capacity because (1) there aren't any U.S. consumer component suppliers to buy parts from, and (2) given the strong yen Japanese VCR components are much too uncompetitive considering what the final price of the machine has to be in the U.S.

Thus Toshiba set up two joint ventures with Samsung in Korea. The first is a firm that produces VCR components for Toshiba's U.S. factory. The second is a firm that assembles VCRs in Korea and exports them to the United States under Toshiba's label. The second will enable Toshiba to continue supplying competitive VCRs to the U.S. market until the components joint venture (JV) can prop up Toshiba's U.S. factory.

As reported, this arrangement benefits all three countries. The United States gains because eventually, with the flow of components from Korea, the U.S.–based Toshiba factory can step up production, meaning more jobs for Americans. Japan gains because the setup provides effective means to counter the strong yen and the fact that one cannot buy competitive consumer components in the United States. Korea gains because, as mentioned earlier, component technology is the Achilles' heel of the Korean manufacturing structure, and the arrangement allows Samsung to acquire that know-how. And, finally, American consumers will still be able to purchase Japanese VCRs without a significant price hike.

Of course, there are many unanswered questions about deals of this sort. Is there any connection between this deal and the Toshiba-COCOM affair? How does Toshiba keep Samsung from using the component technology on its own-label machines and competing in the U.S. market at the finished-goods level? Is the components JV a captive supplier to Toshiba, or can it perhaps sell to the Japanese VCR manufacturer base? Knowing the Japanese, I'm sure they've worked all this into the agreements; that's probably going to be kept under wraps. But, even with all of these unanswered questions, I still feel that the potential is there for the setup to be synergistic to all three countries.

There are many other types of partnership arrangements that accrue positive-sum benefits to all three nations. The three-way partnership among Ford, Mazda, and Kia, in which Mazda designs, Kia manufactures, and Ford sells low-end, market-creating automobiles, is an example. Firms in other three-way partnerships contribute functional expertise in a slightly different manner. The U.S. firm might design and develop, the Japanese firm perform complex manufacturing, and the Korean firm perform relatively simple manufacturing.

It's easy to be quite skeptical about these arrangements, particularly about how they may affect competition. Yet, following a couple of guidelines can allay those anxieties. First, try to structure the arrangement so that the resulting product creates a new market. A product such as the previously mentioned read-only VCR is a complementary product to the Japanese market. People who would have been content with one VCR are now buying a second. The Sony Walkman is another example of such a complementary, nonsubstituting product. Second, make sure that the know-how transferred into the arrangement is controlled and limited to a category of technology not considered to be the most sensitive for the originating firm. This may sound obvious, but many firms neglect to parcel the different technology categories, thus allowing indirect leakage of advanced know-how. Third, structure the partnership correctly, giving consideration to business merit, power balance, and exit costs over time, and devote enough resources to manage the partnership as mentioned in chapter 7. If these factors are carefully considered, there is no limit to the number of creative, positive-sum partnerships that can be established and managed.

Diversification of One's Risks and Dependencies

Nowadays it seems that no country is totally self-sufficient, no matter how hard it tries. The drive toward self-sufficiency is always motivated because one tries to attain peace of mind against possible breakages in dependency. It is quite interesting in view of the trilateral relationship that much economic dependency is concentrated on a few factors, and that diversification needs to be pursued much more aggressively by all three countries.

As one looks at the triangular relationship among the three countries, one interesting observation could be made. In previous chapters, it was noted that Korea has diversified its sourcing of technology so that in the worst case, if one country were to shut off its technology flow, Korea wouldn't be immobilized. One Achilles' heel that Korea is working on today is to diversify the sources of its components and equipment from mainly Japan to the United States, Europe, and itself. Another important dependency that Korea would wish to diversify quickly is its concentration of exports to the U.S. marketplace.

When one looks at all the Japanese subcontracting arrangements in Korea, including the Toshiba-Samsung example mentioned earlier, the Japanese seem to be very resourceful when it comes to diversifying their operations, particularly recently in view of the strong appreciation of the yen and various potential trade sanctions. The Japanese today are not as serious about technology acquisition as the Koreans are, mainly because they are much more advanced, and because they have so much internal technology-generation capability. Clearly, another Japanese weakness is dependency of its export marketplace on the United States. It needs to expand its domestic market or embark on exporting more to markets that are admittedly more difficult to penetrate than is the United States.

The United States has done a reasonable job of diversifying its markets. First, the U.S. domestic market is large; the number of households there is much larger than in Japan or Korea, for example. Second, America's export markets are quite diversified. Ironically, the reason American firms aren't more serious about getting into the Japanese market (compared to the Japanese effort to penetrate the U.S. market) is that most of them can survive without doing so. In other words, the general U.S. perception is that the domestic and European markets will do just fine. Clearly, a very short-term but understandable position.

In the area of technology, American firms have traditionally done a superb job of developing basic technologies and revolutionary products or services. Here again, the blend of an idea-encouraging culture and a large domestic marketplace whose needs stimulate new products and services is the factor behind this success. Yet, in the process of feeling proud of one's accomplishments in this arena, one's NIH ("not invented here," or inability to accept and adopt ideas generated elsewhere) factor starts to include not only basic developmental know-how but also applications, operational, and commercialization know-how. In this sense the United States is quite lopsided; the Japanese have these types of expertise, and American firms should tap them aggressively, since sooner or later follow-on product success will depend heavily on understanding how customers use the product and how to make and commercialize the product. In this sense, the United States should diversify the sources of its know-how more.

However, the most serious U.S. overdependence problem is unrelated to these. In the Korean and Japanese cases of overdependence, the respective governments are well aware of the problem and are taking sometimes effective, sometimes ineffective, steps toward correction. Perhaps the most striking dependency in all of this is the degree to which the United States relies on Japan with respect to the supply of components, equipment, and finished goods. It is easy to threaten the Japanese by feigning protection or even an embargo on their products. However, that would shut down most U.S. industrial manufacturers in about three months. The Japanese, while their culture and good judgment prevent them from stating this bluntly, know that this is the case, and that given the power balance, the United States will always have to compromise down from their retaliatory threats. Whether the United States faces up to it or not, the situation is basically a nonmilitary version of MAD (mutually assured destruction) if one side does anything extreme. Indeed, this is quite a dangerous situation not only for these two countries but for the world.

In the semiconductor industry there is a concept known as second sourcing. Many users of semiconductors make it a policy to endeavor to use second-source products. A second-source product is one that is available from at least two different manufacturers. This provides the user two important benefits: (1) continuity of supply in case one supplier cannot deliver; and (2) some "peace of mind" that if one supplier acts unreasonably with respect to pricing, for example, the other could be engaged more aggressively. This arrangement certainly boosts purchaser power at the expense of supplier power, since the purchaser can play the two suppliers off against each other.

Today U.S. customers, both industrial and consumer, are often in a sole-source position, in the sense that if something catastrophic happened to the Japanese economy, the U.S. economy would be in serious trouble. In the extreme, remember that Tokyo, where a large fraction of the Japanese economy resides, is said to be due for a big earthquake. And let us superimpose one other important factor mentioned in chapter 1. If the reader can accept the view that Japanese culture is quite different and distant from that of the United States, then what one finds is that U.S. customers are in a sole-source, thus very dependent, position with a supplier base that is perhaps one of the hardest in the world to deal with from the standpoint of having totally different value and ethics systems. I'm sure that U.S. government and private-sector negotiators experienced in negotiations with the Japanese will identify with this. Just recently, the chief of the Asian bureau of the Japanese foreign ministry stated in a Japanese television interview that it does seem that the Americans have an easier time understanding the Koreans than the Japanese, since the Koreans tend to display their emotions and to be somewhat more straightforward. And, remember, the driving factor behind this is that the Koreans were forced repeatedly in their history to deal with foreigners, whereas Japanese history is in stark contrast with respect to this point. Thus, America is finding it challenging to deal with the Japanese; Korea is finding it challenging to deal with the Japanese; and America is finding it relatively easier to deal with the Koreans.

Let's add this all up. Korea is a country that has modeled a significant amount of its development strategy on the

Japanese experience. One important aspect of this is that the products in which Korea is becoming competitive are very similar to those in which the Japanese are competitive—namely, steel, cars, consumer electronics, and now semiconductors. Korea's culture at least feels easier to the Americans. These two factors put together represent a tremendous opportunity for the United States to develop a second source for the products that are currently sole-sourced from Japan so that it can play Japan off against Korea and vice versa. Of course, where it can, the United States should strive to regain competitiveness, but in arenas where U.S.-based production is structurally uneconomical, alternate sourcing has to be the only way really to play hardball against Japan, compared to empty retaliatory threats. For example, whereas it may be worthwhile for the United States to consider becoming competitive in high-end color TVs, production of low-end TVs in the United States would be rather uneconomical, and therefore one might as well increase the purchasing power of these latter products through alternate sourcing.

Yet it seems that taking a short-term view, the United States is threatening to "go after Korea" in view of the trade deficits it is incurring. Recent moves include many of the same tactics used with the Japanese, and due to preemption, Korea is having to deal with these tactics much earlier in its development cycle than Japan did. This strategy is unbelievably short-term in perspective and not very effective at that. According to KDI projections, Korea is "peanuts" compared to Japan today or in the year 2000, and instead of seizing an opportunity that arose from historical coincidence to develop a second source, slowing down Korea's growth would not only debilitate an important adjustment mechanism for Japan and the United States but also just about guarantee that the United States will continue to be heavily dependent on Japanese manufacturers and the skills of the U.S. negotiators to work out significant differences over and over again. And this is not even to mention the prospects of Korea's defaulting on its U.S. loans, the consequences of which would also be quite adverse to U.S. financial institutions.

I'm sure that all of the above sounds quite unfavorable to Japan. I do not intend it in that way. In fact, I have lived in Japan for quite a few years, and as this book represents, I have come to respect many aspects of the Japanese people. I have many close Japanese friends. Yet, having personally made the cultural adjustment between Japan and the United States twice in my life, I know better than most how polar the two cultures are.

At times in the course of history, partners whose values are extremely different are better off in a relationship with greater breathing room than total dependency would allow. Such dependency requires both partners to interact intensely, and doing so with polar values creates friction. It is perhaps better for Japan to not have to shoulder the heavy responsibility that comes from being a sole source for many products to the U.S. marketplace.

Also, in my experience with Japan, I've found that external pressure has always brought out the best from the Japanese in terms of adjustment. (The same can be said about Korea in certain arenas.) Fear motivates Japanese organizations to change dramatically, and unfortunately, very little else can have the same effect. As trade friction has in ways prompted Japan to adjust, more intense competition with NIEs such as Korea will additionally prompt Japan to integrate foreign values into the Japanese environment. This will undoubtedly reduce the cultural distance between Japan and its economic allies.

Now, let me offer some recommendations. Allow Korea to develop as rapidly as possible, not necessarily to help out the Korean people but to position the United States more securely. When Korea gets to the point at which (in the industries in which it is competitive) it has enough capacity to act as a second source for Japan, play the two countries off against one another in terms of the procurement of those products that the United States finds uneconomical to produce locally. So, at the government level, encourage Korea to develop as rapidly as possible by offering aid, and even if that is not possible, the least one can do is not to get in the way of the Koreans' development. While I know that quite a few U.S. firms have already become involved with the Koreans, I would urge every American company that has partnered with or purchased from Japanese firms seriously to consider a similar arrangement with the Koreans. If such diversification could occur at both the public- and private-sector levels, the United States would be much better positioned in the medium-to-long term.

I would describe Korea's future as carefully optimistic. Korea has managed to maneuver through narrow straits to reach the economic state it is at today. While Korea still has a long way to go, its experience is already being studied by less-developed countries. Perhaps, this "success" so far is the result of the survival instinct gained through two millennia of turmoil.

I believe that the triangular relationship among Korea, the United States, and Japan can be made to work. Many win-win, synergistic arrangements could be set up. Also, some prudent diversification can go a long way toward alleviating the current friction that exists between the countries. Korea is already playing and can continue to play a critical role in the adjustments that the United States and Japan are going through. With rational thinking by all three countries, significant value can be added to the world economy through trilateral synergy. As an optimist when it comes to the world's ability to improve over time, I trust that rationality, not emotion, will prevail in the end. The stakes are getting too big for flippant emotion.

Such rational relationship-building by the United States and Japan is the way in which Korea will survive and prosper. By the same token, irrationality on the part of any one of the three countries will mean disaster for Korea and a significant negative impact for the aggressor. But, given some of Korea's skills—namely, the abilities to turn change to one's advantage and to negotiate favorably from a position of weakness—it is at least as reasonable to speculate that the Korean economy will continue to survive and grow as it has in the past as it is to be pessimistic about future prospects.

If this projection is accurate, Korea will mean a lot of opportunities as a market and as a partner for many U.S., European, and Japanese firms. I am sure that as time passes, there will be more vigorous discussion on Korean industry and firms, as there was on Japanese industry and firms. I hope this book serves as one of the first steps in such understanding.

Index